D0103677

# the series on school r

| | | |
|---|---|---|
| **Patricia A. Wasley** | **Ann Lieberman** | **Joseph P. McDonald** |
| University | Carnegie Foundation for the | New York |
| of Washington | Advancement of Teaching | University |

**SERIES EDITORS**

*(Continued)*

## the series on school reform, *continued*

# GOING TO SCALE
## WITH
# NEW SCHOOL DESIGNS

## REINVENTING HIGH SCHOOL

*Joseph P. McDonald*
*Emily J. Klein*
*Meg Riordan*

TEACHERS
COLLEGE
PRESS

Teachers College
Columbia University
New York and London

Published by Teachers College Press, 1234 Amsterdam Avenue, New York, NY 10027

*Library of Congress Cataloging-in-Publication Data*

McDonald, Joseph P.
  Going to scale with new school designs : reinventing high school / Joseph P. McDonald, Emily J. Klein, Meg Riordan.
      p. cm. — (the series on school reform)
  Includes bibliographical references and index.
  ISBN 978-0-8077-4986-9 (pbk. : alk. paper) —ISBN 978-0-8077-4987-6 (hardcover : alk. paper)
  1. High school facilities—United States—Planning.  2. High school buildings—United States—Design and construction.  3. High school environment—United States.  4. School improvement programs—United States.  I. Klein, Emily J.  II. Riordan, Meg. III. Title.
  LB3209.M38 2009
  373.16—dc22

                                                                      2009012074

ISBN 978-0-8077-4986-9 (paperback)
ISBN 978-0-8077-4987-6 (hardcover)

Printed on acid-free paper
Manufactured in the United States of America

16  15  14  13  12  11  10  09      8  7  6  5  4  3  2  1

*for Beth*
*—JPM*

*for Barbara and Jerry Klein*
*—EJK*

*for Andrew*
*—MR*

# Contents

# GOING TO SCALE
## WITH
# NEW SCHOOL DESIGNS

# 1

# Introduction

It was not until the early 1990s that the phenomenon we discuss in this book became imaginable. The United States has been preoccupied with school reform—especially high school reform—since the mid-19th century, and questions of how school reform spreads and of what *spread* really means have long been of interest. But hardly anyone before the early 1990s thought of school reform in terms of creating new and multiple school designs, and "going to scale" with them—that is, replicating them many times in different contexts. By that time, however, the United States had experienced nearly a decade of school "restructuring"—particularly high school restructuring. Propelled by a powerful critique of the American high school captured in several widely read and influential texts, the restructuring effort aimed implicitly to produce a new standard design.

The most widely read and influential of these texts was the 1983 report of the National Commission on Excellence in Education, called *A Nation at Risk*. Also influential and widely read were John Goodlad's (1984) *A Place Called School*, Ernest Boyer's (1985) *High School*, Ted Sizer's (1984) *Horace's Compromise*, and Arthur Powell, David Cohen, and Eleanor Farrar's (1985) *The Shopping Mall High School*. The restructuring effort was full of political struggle—particularly within schools themselves—but had minimal impact beyond new design ideas and some design exemplars. A few veterans of the effort, among them some people highlighted in this book, wanted by the early 1990s to try another approach. This involved moving away from standard design and embracing multiple designs. It also seized an opportunity created by a growing worldwide tendency to apply market thinking and market mechanisms to social services.

In 1990, for example, John Chubb and Terry Moe rescued Milton Friedman's 35-year-old idea about giving families vouchers to buy the schooling they wanted instead of assigning children to particular government-operated schools (Friedman, 1955; Moe, 2001). In 1991, Minnesota passed the nation's first law authorizing charter schools, hailed then and now by its proponents as a "supply-side" innovation fostering a more equitable schooling market (Nathan, 1999; Viteritti, 1999). That same year, the New American Schools Development Corporation was launched. It promised the development of "break the mold" comprehensive school designs by not-for-profit school designers and the marketing of these designs to districts (Berends, Bodilly, & Kirby, 2002; Glennan, 1998). In 1997, Congress passed a law known as the Obey-Porter legislation (named after its congressional sponsors), which helped build the market for such designs by offering up to $50,000 each year for 3 years to schools willing to adopt one (Keltner, 1998). In 1993, Edison Schools, led by a former president of Yale University, opened for business as a for-profit school designer, one prepared to work with charters or districts. By the end of the decade, voucher systems had been launched in Milwaukee, Cleveland, and Florida, and charter schools were in operation nearly everywhere, often designed and run by not-for-profit or for-profit entities called charter management organizations.

By then, too, many school districts had begun to outsource operations previously undertaken in-house, contracting not only for lunch and transportation services, but also for curriculum and professional development tied to the curriculum. It would not be long before they were contracting as well for school management, including management by design. Today, major school districts like New York City, Chicago, and Philadelphia are described as "mixed systems," whereby school choice coexists with school assignment, city-supported charter schools compete with their more regulated counterparts, market and bureaucratic jargons intermingle, and schooling by design—in particular, high schooling by design—has become common, if not yet commonplace.

Thus questions that concern us in this book became important:

- How should third-party proprietary designers of schooling go about installing and supporting their design in many different contexts?
- What challenges should the designers expect to meet in the process?
- How best can the designers manage these challenges?
- What should their clients expect?
- What roles must both be prepared to play?

These questions have few direct antecedents in educational inquiry. They sound more like business questions because they *are* business questions. This fact has not been lost on funders of the new design work, especially the Bill and Melinda Gates Foundation, which began to invest heavily in new high school design and its replication in the 1st decade of the 21st century. Nor was it lost on the authors of this book when another foundation (which wishes to remain anonymous because it does not usually fund such work) commissioned us in 2002 to try to answer the questions above through a close study of a high school designer that Gates had just funded.

The designer is known today as Big Picture Learning but was then called the Big Picture Company. In 1996, it opened a small and different kind of high school in a corridor of the Rhode Island State Department of Education in Providence. Today, it oversees a network of more than 60 Big Picture schools nationwide with more under development. In studying the effort of the Big Picture to go to scale with its new high school design, we also studied high schooling in general and what schooling by design can do for it.

## ABOUT BIG PICTURE LEARNING

Big Picture Learning is a nonprofit education reform organization head-quartered in Providence, Rhode Island. It was founded in 1995 by Dennis Littky and Elliot Washor, experienced educators and adventurous educational entrepreneurs. Littky was founding principal in 1972 of the Shoreham–Wading River Middle School on Long Island, New York. In her 1984 book about exemplary middle schools, Joan Lipsitz calls Littky "the red-bearded rebel" (p. 155). At about the time the Lipsitz book appeared, however, Littky had become a graying rebel who was about to be fired from his next job as principal of Thayer Junior-Senior High School in Winchester, New Hampshire. He was fired by a school board uncomfortable with his innovations, but then reinstated in a dramatic turn of events chronicled by Susan Kammeraad-Campbell in her 1989 book, *Doc*, and then in the 1992 NBC-TV movie derived from the book, *A Town Torn Apart*. Littky stayed at Thayer for more than a decade after his reinstatement and helped make the school an exemplar of late-20th-century high school reform as a charter member of Ted Sizer's Coalition of Essential Schools.

Elliot Washor had worked closely with Littky on Long Island, then joined him in his later years at Thayer, where he produced an early reality TV show called *Here, Thayer, and Everywhere*. It played a role in disseminating design ideas across the Coalition of Essential Schools, as well as other reform networks, and it also stimulated both men's interest in new design adventures. Washor and Littky moved to Rhode Island in the early 1990s at the invitation of the Annenberg Institute for School Reform at Brown University, then headed by Sizer. They came determined to go beyond the bounds of the reforms they had achieved in their previous work together. Thus they were among the people we mentioned above—restructuring reform veterans who wanted to rethink the restructuring approach. The

Big Picture Company was the product of this rethinking, and it was incubated at the Annenberg Institute. Its first project was to design a different kind of high school for Providence—different physically, different in its curriculum, and different in its relationship with the city and the state. The result was the Met, a high school that opened in 1996 as a state-supported school. The name stands for the Metropolitan Regional Career and Technical Center. It was designed to enable students to discover and follow passionate interests through "real-world" learning. Each student is immersed 2 whole days a week in a community of adults working in the same area of interest, mentored closely and on a voluntary basis by one of the adults. For the rest of the week, in an environment more like a design studio than a classroom, and with coaching from an advisor (who works with roughly a dozen other students too), the student pursues projects in accordance with an individualized learning plan. The advisor, varied mentors the student takes on over his or her years at the Met, and the student's family collaborate to develop successive plans and monitor the student's learning progress toward the achievement of the school's overall learning goals. All Met students are pressed to apply to college and to attend, and many take college courses while still at the Met, for example, at nearby Rhode Island Community College. Elliot Levine's (2002) book about the Met, *One Kid at a Time: Big Lessons from a Small School*, is a good source for learning more about the Met.

The larger mission of Big Picture (BP) is to generate and support educational institutions that tailor their work to the unique interests and qualities of the people they educate and that also situate learning to the greatest possible extent in the real-world workplaces of their communities (www.bigpicture.org). To this end, BP provides designs, professional education, school coaching, and other kinds of assistance to K–12 schools, colleges, networks of schools, a network of youth organizations creating schools, and individual educators. Still, it is best known today for the Met (currently with six locations in Providence, five in the city's poorest neighborhood) and for the national network of BP schools that replicate the Met, 63 of them as of 2008, in 16 states and the District of Columbia (with additional schools in Australia, Israel, and the Netherlands). These schools are not directly operated by BP (except in Providence), nor are they franchises in the ordinary sense. They operate independently under memoranda of understanding between BP and districts or charter management organizations, and they use BP designs and other assistance. The provision of assistance has been supported by grants from the Bill and Melinda Gates Foundation and other sources. While the original Met is still located in a corridor of the Rhode Island Department of Education, the other five Met locations are new buildings that were constructed to BP specifications under

BP direction. Elliot Washor, who served as general overseer of this construction project, captures the important physical side of new school design in a 2003 online book about this project. His book plus Dennis Littky's (2004) are the best sources for tracking BP's intellectual roots.

Liberated from the task of restructuring the conventional American high school, Littky, Washor, and their colleagues imagined a high school design that would prove particularly attractive to youth who find themselves unattracted for various reasons to the conventional design. This may be because it seems to them too constraining, boring, impersonal, excessively "academic," or incapable of dealing successfully with their unique interests and needs. In his 2004 book, Littky reverses the order of what some high school reformers, including the Bill and Melinda Gates Foundation, call the new three "R's": rigor, relevance, and relationships (Daggett, 2005; McNulty & Quaglia, 2007; Weeks, 2003). He begins with relationships (those between adults and youth, and school and family), suggesting that these are fundamental to the others (see also Washor & Mojkowski, 2006/ 2007). He adds that relevance can best be achieved through work-focused, community-based learning. And he finishes with rigor, which he associates with opportunities for intense concentration in a challenging area of great interest. Such opportunities, say Mihaly Csikszentmihalyi and Barbara Schneider (2000), are characteristic of the early formative experiences of creative and productive people.

BP school students, as we mentioned above, spend at least 2 full days a week in an experience BP calls Learning Through Internship, or LTI. Here they may work with a photographer, a medical technician, a police officer, a TV producer, or some other mentor whom the students themselves have often helped to locate while pursuing some strong interest (one that may shift or change as they mature). The rest of the week they learn under the tutelage of an advisor within an advisory of roughly a dozen other students. Conferring with the student's family in the process, the advisor helps each advisee craft a unique Learning Plan tied to the interest explored in the LTI and designed to meet Learning Goals within five broad domains:

- Communication
- Empirical reasoning
- Quantitative reasoning
- Social reasoning
- Personal qualities (respect, responsibility, organization, leadership, reflection, and striving)

On a quarterly basis, students are assessed on their progress in meeting these goals by means of public exhibitions of project-based work they have completed. For one of her quarterly projects, a student interning at an organic farm built a garden that replicated the farm on a small scale. To meet her quantitative reasoning goal, she devised an Excel database to keep track of the farm's crops. She incorporated historical data in the database and analyzed trends. For empirical reasoning she looked at whether moon phases affected seed germination rates. For social reasoning, she conducted research into community-supported agriculture, its history, and arguments for and against it.

The quarterly exhibitions are chaired by advisors and attended by other students as well as parents, mentors, and sometimes guests. Advisors prompt the exhibitors to step back from their work and answer such questions as "What have you learned about yourself?" "What problems did you encounter and how did you overcome them?" and "What would you change about your work to improve it?" Following each exhibition, students receive lengthy written narratives from the advisor reviewing the exhibition with the Learning Plans and Goals in mind.

Intellectually, the BP design is rooted in John Dewey's complex ideas about the role of interest and experience in education, in particular, his ideas about what makes an interest educative (he thought it was its connection to a larger world of experience), about the role of expert guidance in the pursuit of an interest (he thought it crucial), and about the important role of practical activity in the process (also crucial) (Dewey, 1938/1997). As both Littky's (2004) and Washor's (2003) books make clear, BP taps these Deweyan roots directly, and through the work of other thinkers and writers. Among these others are some who urge more patience than educators or educational policymakers generally show for the natural development that derives from just growing up among caring and thoughtful adults. These thinkers and writers include the school-rooted reformers Ted Sizer (1984, 2004) and Deborah Meier (2002), the insightful reform skeptic Seymour Sarason (1972, 1982, 1995), the deschooling advocate Ivan Illich (1971), and the home schooling advocate John Holt (1964, 1967). Other writers and thinkers who have helped to shape BP's ideas and practices include advocates for the role of hands-on thinking and learning. Among them are the 20th-century Italian educator Maria Montessori (1966), the Stanford neurologist Frank R. Wilson (1998), the cognitive psychologist Roger Schank (2000), and National Public Radio's *Car Talk* star Tom Magliozzi (Magliozzi & Magliozzi, 2000).

Trust in development plus emphasis on hands-on learning make the BP curriculum far more experiential than the typical high school curriculum. At any given moment, a student in a BP school is much more likely than a student in a conventional high school to be active with his or her hands, to be moving about rather than sitting down, to be working outside rather than inside a classroom or school building, to be initiating a project of his or her own design, and to be working beside adults. This also means that he or she is less likely—at quarterly intervals, say—to have covered some specified amount of content knowledge. Indeed, BP is deeply skeptical about the intellectual and developmental value of the kind of content frameworks and time lines that are highly characteristic of American schooling, and it is wary of the kind of content auditing that constitutes much of American educational accountability. BP believes instead in the power over time of the three R's—*relationships, relevance*, and *rigor* (as defined above)—to help young people grow up and, in the process, become smarter, more literate, and more knowledgeable in ways that connect them successfully to the world and the world's occupations and that make them more morally attuned to others and society. It chooses therefore to be accountable in terms of other markers of progress: Does the student who hated school come to like it? Does the student develop and sustain intellectual interests? Does the student grow perceptibly—in the view of his or her mentors, teachers, and family—in the five broad domains of learning bulleted above? Does the student stay in school? Does the student apply to college, get into college, and stay in college?

Of course, BP functions within a policy climate that relies principally on other measures of educational progress than these—not just for individual students, but for schools, educational management organizations, and school designers. The other measures especially include standardized tests tied to disciplinary content frameworks. Given the dominant influence of such tests—and in consideration of BP's ideas and unconventional practices—it seems quite remarkable at first to learn that there is even *one* BP school operating in the United States today, let alone more than 60. The fact that there *are* more than 60 is partly a testament to BP's political skills in the face of the scale-up challenges we discuss in this book, though it is surely a testament also to the fact that BP does not aim to be a new standard high school. It aims instead to serve those who are most dissatisfied with that standard—a group that in urban areas constitutes nearly half of all youth as measured by the dropout rate.

The Gates Foundation divides all its school design grantees into three groups. The first group—called "traditional"—includes designers such as Aspire Public Schools, Knowledge Is Power (KIPP), and Early College High School. They have created schools that are *different* in some of the ways we use the term in this book. For the most part, however, they are not different in the content of their curricula. Gates says they teach traditional subjects but in ways that prepare all their students to succeed in learning them well. Such school designers make an important contribution to high schooling. As we argue in Chapter 6, however, the portfolio of high school designs necessary to prepare all American youth well for higher education and the 21st-century workplace will also have to include designs that take other paths to intellectual development, that operate on the basis of an epistemology less tied to traditional academic disciplines. Gates apparently agrees, and thus its second group of funded designers—which it calls "theme-based" designers—argue for different curriculum content too. For example, High Tech High weaves pre-engineering throughout the curriculum, transforming it in the process. Expeditionary Learning Schools puts character development on a par with academic development to similar effect. The third group of Gates-funded designers—which the foundation calls "student-centered"—includes BP, as well as Diploma Plus, YouthBuild Schools, and several others. These designers, as Gates puts it, "create individualized plans for each student, often with students' input, and may focus especially on drop-outs or at-risk youth" (www.gatesfoundation.org). Following Gates and other funders, many policymakers make room for such radical high school designers because they take on the toughest cases.

We must add, however, that the network of BP schools continues to grow because the schools' cumulative record—even on conventional content-focused achievement measures—is good when matched with an appropriate comparison group. It is also because the record is exceptionally good with respect to conventional measures of progress that BP itself targets, namely, attendance, graduation rates, and college-going rates. More about how BP schools measure up in Chapter 6.

## HOW WE STUDIED BIG PICTURE GOING TO SCALE

We are educational researchers—we would unabashedly say *school* researchers—and we knew that we would have a lot to learn about taking a business perspective on BP's efforts to start other BP schools. We were, nonetheless, eager for the adventure. One of us (McDonald) had written about BP earlier, and he was interested in how it had developed in the intervening years (Walker & McDonald, 1996). He has long been interested in high school reform generally, but particularly in efforts that make high schooling more intellectually powerful *and* less academically narrow. This is the design task that BP especially set for itself. At the time, McDonald had also just completed a study of the National Writing Project as part of a larger study by the Rand Corporation of going to scale with school reforms, and he wondered about the applicability of the Rand findings to the BP case (Glennan, Bodilly, Galegher, & Kerr, 2004; McDonald, Buchanan, & Sterling, 2004). Meanwhile, the other two authors of this book were then beginning their now-completed doctoral studies. One (Riordan) was interested—for reasons traceable in her own education and teaching career (and now in her postdoctoral career path)—in the role of experiential learning in school design (Riordan, 2006). Of course, the BP design puts a heavy emphasis on experiential learning. The other author (Klein) was interested in the role that professional development plays in replications of successful educational practices. To what extent, she wondered, was replicating a school design all about professionals learning the design (Klein, 2005)?

By 2001, BP had already replicated the Met once and was in the process of building the campus that would house four more replications. Taking notice, the Bill and Melinda Gates Foundation asked BP if it wanted to try the same thing in places beyond Rhode Island. As we began our study, BP was building new schools in five other states. We followed this work closely for the next 3 years. In the process, we discovered that while the questions that guided our study (bulleted above) begin in economics, they also involve politics. Of course, readers more familiar than we were then with business reform literature could have told us so. The good news in this for readers of this book is that politics makes good stories, in this case, stories of challenge and response to challenge, of conflict meeting invention, and of unexpected opportunity and transformation.

Of course, if you only wanted interesting stories, you'd have bought a book of fiction rather than this book. But we believe that our stories and the other material that make up this book are relevant as well as interesting—broadly relevant to education. Although our research focused on one high school reform effort, our findings apply, through a process we describe below, to reform at other levels of schooling too, and to reform that focuses more on policy, curriculum, or pedagogy than on school design. At the 1993 White House announcement of Walter Annenberg's half-billion-dollar gift to American school reform, President Bill Clinton declared that all the problems besetting American education had already been solved somewhere and that the trick was to find out where and then to get the solutions to travel. His "travel" is another name for "going to scale."

We conducted our research using conventional social science methods that included observations, interviews, document collection and review, electronic data storage and analysis, and triangulation of data sources as a basis for drawing conclusions. However, we mixed these methods with somewhat less conventional ones that have had an impact on the book. For one thing, we presented findings iteratively in four essays written while we were still collecting data (McDonald, Klein, & Riordan, 2003a, 2003b, 2004a, 2004b). We called them *essays* with the French root of the word in mind: *essai*, meaning "an attempt." Each attempted to capture a complex and shifting phenomenon. We named strategies we were seeing in BP's work, and from the strategies we inferred the challenges these strategies addressed, eventually enumerating seven of them (plus one more that we reveal in the book). We did all this in dialogue with BP designers, using the successive essays (as well as drafts of them) to conduct this dialogue. We also circulated the essays among a small mix of other school designers, school reformers, policymakers, and funders—including our own funder. We asked them whether the challenges we were naming seemed plausible to them as challenges applicable beyond the BP case. We were of course *not* suggesting that research findings based on a single school designer's experience could be regarded as generalizable to other designers in the ordinary sense of the word. We were fishing instead for what Chris Argyris and Donald Schön (1996) call "reflective transfer."

Reflective transfer happens when parties working in a somewhat parallel situation to one that has been carefully documented and analyzed say how their situation is both like and unlike the situation presented. In the process, they gain greater insight into their own situation and, possibly, gain access as well to strategies adaptable to their own situation. We encouraged this reflective transfer in our essays through analogy. The essays were laced with analogy, as is this book. Some instances involve *close-in* analogy, for example, between BP and other school designers, especially Expeditionary Learning Schools, or between BP and other educational reform organizations such as the National Writing Project. Still others involve *big-stretch* analogy, for example, between BP and the performance artists collectively known as Blue Man Group, or BP and Whole Foods supermarkets, or BP and Starbucks. Moreover, we take two big-stretch analogies to considerable length, what literary analysts would call *conceit*, though what we call a *distant mirror*. One comes at the end of Chapter 3 and the other at the end of Chapter 4. Like most of our other big-stretch analogies, they are drawn from a field of interest you're likely to find quite familiar, namely, food. We thought that a single and familiar contrasting human service focus might enhance the power of our analogies to induce reflective transfer (and might also make the writing and the reading more fun). Thus you will read in this book not only about high schools and other kinds of educational settings, but also about restaurants and grocery stores, and about bread, olive oil, ice cream, and coffee. Bon appétit!

We have also aimed to capture in the book a facsimile of the dialogue that surrounded the essays as we circulated them and discussed them with others. It takes the form of a kind of hypertext composed of comments on the main text by two early readers. We call them our *dialogue partners*. In order to help us prompt your reflective transfer, we've asked them to say how the BP experience in going to scale is both like and unlike their own experiences in going to scale. Their comments are threaded through the book. Mimicking the interplay of different kinds of analogies, one of these dialogue partners is an educational entrepreneur, and the other is a food entrepreneur.

## Another School Designer

Our first dialogue partner is Greg Farrell, founding designer and recently retired president and CEO of Expeditionary Learning Schools. ELS was one of the school design efforts launched by the New American Schools Project (mentioned above as a progenitor of schooling by design). Today there are more than 150 Expeditionary Learning schools in the United States, urban, rural, and suburban and divided equally among elementary, middle, and high schools.

ELS grew out of the Education/Urban Initiative of Outward Bound, the international outdoor education program for people of all ages. The German-born educator Kurt Hahn founded Outward Bound in Wales in 1941 (Flavin, 1996). Hahn believed that placing people in challenging outdoor situations helps them gain confidence, redefine their perceptions of their abilities, demonstrate compassion, and develop a spirit of camaraderie with their peers. In an Outward Bound course, Farrell explains, "you get really fit, but you do so in order to have fitness left over to help someone else." The ELS design principles follow Hahn's insistence on the integration of academic and character development. The core idea, Farrell says, is that "there is a kind of redeeming social and moral purpose to schools that has to do not only with discovering you can be more than you thought, but in turning your power to the help of others." The ELS catchword is "Crew, not passengers," and it comes right out of Hahn. Farrell explains:

> In the Outward Bound experience, you're used to sleeping on the ground and not asking for a lot of service. You're more into giving. Furthermore, sleeping on the ground is fun—that's the attitude you want. We're going whether it rains or not! No one is a passenger— we're all pitching in and helping out. This is the cultural foundation of the design's blend of academics and character.

At the heart of the ELS design is a core practice called Learning Expeditions. "We try to do as much of the curriculum as possible," Farrell says, "through these long, deep studies of something." A Learning Expedition is built of challenging projects interwoven with reading and writing experiences across the curriculum and is punctuated by performances and exhibitions for real audiences. They always involve fieldwork, Farrell explains, "getting out there someplace and getting into contact with people who *do* this—whatever *this* the expedition is about: politicians, architects, veterans of World War II, or people who run the aquarium." A second core practice is Active Pedagogy—the kind of teaching that an ELS school aims for whether or not an expedition is under way. Active Pedagogy emphasizes inquiry, active engagement rather than passive participation, and rigor defined by authenticity—a relationship to occupational practices in the real world.

As you may notice, the ELS design has some things in common with the BP design, particularly in its attention to the crucial role of direct experience in learning and growing, its habit of finding its reference points in authentic real-world activity rather than academic disciplines alone, its pursuit of learning opportunities outside school, and its reliance on performance-based assessment. However, the designs are different too in important ways. For example, ELS relies on team-based learning experiences, in contrast to BP's greater emphasis on individualized learning. ELS is different as well in its greater accommodation of other kinds of learning milieus and teaching strategies, beyond the ones its design especially highlights. This difference is attributable, Greg Farrell thinks, to differences in how the designers started out. More about this later in the book.

## And a Coffee "Mate"

Our second dialogue partner is Howard Wollner, retired senior vice president of Starbucks, who worked for the company between 1992, when it became a publicly traded company of 165 stores, and 2005, when it had more than 10,000 stores (http://www.starbucks.com/aboutus/company_timeline.pdf). Starbucks was founded in Seattle in 1971 by three young entrepreneurs. They learned about coffee from the Dutch-born Alfred Peet, who had opened a small store 5 years earlier in Berkeley, California, called Peet's Coffee and Tea. Starbucks was at first a kind of northwest outpost of Peet's store, an enthusiastic collaborator in introducing Americans to the mysteries and pleasures of dark-roasted Arabica coffee beans. Like Peet's, the original Starbucks stores were places you went to buy such beans packed by hand, along with equipment like grinders and brewers to turn the beans into beverages. They were not like the Starbucks stores we know today, where the Arabica beans are turned into sometimes exotic beverages before your very eyes and where (in many locations) you can slip onto a comfortable couch with your laptop and drink the beverages right on site. This Starbucks began to develop 10 years later, when Brooklyn-born Howard Schultz, then working for the housewares division of a multinational corporation, wondered why a small Seattle company was ordering more of a certain kind of drip coffeemaker than Macy's was. Schultz traveled to Seattle to investigate, and, as he describes in his 1997 book, *Pour Your Heart into It*, he fell in love with those Arabica beans. He had never tasted such coffee before, and he was sure that few other Americans had. With his marketing skills, he thought, he could help Starbucks get bigger and more influential, both within and beyond Seattle.

Over the course of the next several years, Schultz worked to sell the Starbucks owners on the virtue of going to scale. Eventually, he managed to turn the coffee purveyor into a coffeehouse, and, in time, into an international coffee experience. That transformation began in 1983, when Schultz, then the company's director of retail operations and marketing, experienced an epiphany during a trip to Milan. It was composed of images of corner espresso bars, sounds of daily customers chatting with friendly baristas, and the taste (the first for Schultz) of a café latte. These images of "ritual and romance," as Schultz puts it in his book, struck him also as the keys to a business opportunity (1997, p. 51). The Milano espresso bars that enchanted him supplied for the Milanese something he sensed Americans missed in their own neighborhoods and that they might be persuaded to pay for—at least more than they typically paid in those days for a cup of coffee. Later his intuition found its theoretical mooring in an idea first advanced by Ray Oldenburg (1989, 1991) and explored also by Richard Florida (2002). It concerns the need within an increasingly disconnected society for a "third place" beyond work and home, one where community can form—even the kind of thin but nonetheless comforting community associated with seeing familiar faces in public space. Back home in 1983, however, Schultz found his vision hard to sell to his boss, Starbucks president and co-owner Jerry Baldwin. The latter told him plainly, "Howard, listen to me. It's just not the right thing to do. If we focus too much on serving coffee, we'll become just another restaurant or cafeteria. It may seem reasonable, each step of the way, but in the end we'll lose our coffee roots" (Schultz, 1997, p. 61). Schultz rejected Baldwin's warning (as he would similar warnings from others again and again over the years). However, he eventually won his immediate argument with Baldwin. The win came by a circuitous route that first had Schultz leaving the company in 1985 to start the Italian-inspired coffee bar he envisioned (brewing Starbucks beans and with the help of a Starbucks investment), and led in 1987 to his buying Starbucks. This happened when Baldwin, having already bought out Peet's, decided to focus on it and to put the original Starbucks assets up for sale. Circuitous routes are not unusual in going to scale, where so much depends on seizing opportunity. By the early 1990s, Schultz was ready, as Howard Wollner puts it, to begin engineering the "elevation of coffee from commodity to experience." Wollner was there as the many challenges of turning romance to scale unfolded. And "there was no road map," he recalls. We take his phrase to stand for our purpose in writing this book—to create a kind of road map for going to scale with new school designs.

## CHALLENGES OF GOING TO SCALE

In studying Big Picture, as we said above, we saw its strategies first rather than the challenges the strategies addressed. We understood what the company was doing before we understood why. This is not just because we were slow to see the deeper levels of schooling by design, but because BP was too. For BP, as for the new Starbucks, there was no road map. In the fast-paced world of designing a new kind of high school, action, not mapping, takes precedence. It is action rooted more in instinct and habit than in rational analysis. We saw our work as helping to supply the rational analysis post hoc. This is the old-fashioned way—before global positioning systems—mapping the road *after* you travel it.

In our research, we trusted in a method that attends to both action and intention, what Argyris and Schon (1996) and others call a *theory of action* approach (Schön & McDonald, 1998; Weiss, 1972, 1995). It requires making the people whose work you study partners in the study. As Don Schön liked to say, it involves pursuing these partners as they work, taking "snapshot" after snapshot, holding the results before them, and asking, "Is this what you mean to do?" Then it involves sitting down with them and discussing their perceptions of what the snapshots capture and fail to capture.

In the book, we foreground the challenges we eventually deciphered rather than the strategies we initially perceived. Be aware that this makes the analysis neater than the experience. Books that aim to explain complex things have to do this. However, we believe they should also pause now and then—this is a pause—to acknowledge the messiness they've cleaned up, and the ambiguity and uncertainty they've thereby concealed. Otherwise, such books risk making practice seem foolish, as if it ought to have waited for research to tell it what to do. That said, the BP work going to scale is now mapped out for others to follow or at least learn from. The map shows the swamps and the cliffs.

We found that BP faced eight challenges as it moved from being a school designer operating in one medium-sized city to being a national (and with BP projects now in the Netherlands, Israel, and Australia) an international player in the school design business. (See a list of the challenges below.) The book is organized around the challenges. Thus Chapters 2 and 3 focus on the first five of the challenges—a cluster fundamentally concerned with the relationship between what the design is and how it spreads. Chapter 3 ends with a distant mirror that aims to put these first challenges in a larger perspective. This is why we privately call it the "olive oil chapter." Chapter 4 deals with the Resource Challenge. For reasons of complexity, this needs a whole chapter to itself. We privately call it the "ice cream chapter," again because of the distant mirror we use to gain perspective on the role of resources in going to scale. The Political Challenge needs its own chapter too, so we devote all of Chapter 5 to it. However, we don't write about food in this chapter, since politics is satisfying enough. Politics is also the subject of Chapter 6—a more deep-seated politics that is associated with what we call the Mindset Challenge. It concerns the persistence of ideas about what high school is that are difficult to reconcile with what we say we want high schooling to do, namely, provide *all* American adolescents with an intellectually powerful and economically empowering education.

## Eight Challenges

1. *Fidelity Challenge.* Balancing fidelity and adaptation.
2. *Teaching Challenge.* Teaching and learning the design.
3. *Ownership Challenge.* Instilling shared ownership of the design.
4. *Communication Challenge.* Communicating effectively across contexts.
5. *Feedback Challenge.* Using experience in new settings to improve the design.
6. *Resource Challenge.* Obtaining and managing resources.
7. *Political Challenge.* Negotiating the politics of local adoption.
8. *Mindset Challenge.* Coping with the difference that difference makes.

In Chapter 7, we summarize all eight challenges as well as our advice in how to address them. This is the complete road map (though it doesn't fold out).

## ACKNOWLEDGMENTS

We begin by thanking the foundation that (anonymously) funded the bulk of our research. We also thank the Spencer Foundation, which provided assistance. The Spencer grant enabled us to plumb the literature on urban high schooling and to review carefully the proceedings of a Spencer-sponsored conference on studying the urban high school held in New York City in May 2001. Of course, we thank the Big Picture Company, and its network of schools, which opened itself to our research in extraordinary ways. We are especially indebted to those who helped us organize our study: Dennis Littky, Elliot Washor, Samantha Broun, Molly Schen, Martha

Cook, Elliot Levine, Elayne Walker Cabral, Joe Battaglia, Rachel Brian, and Charlie Mojkowski.

We especially thank our dialogue partners, Greg Farrell and Howard Wollner, for agreeing to join us in this unusual writing project. The book is far more valuable for their contributions. We thank as well other people who helped with this project along the way. They include Pat Wasley, Carole Saltz, Amy Gerstein, Ann Bowers, Nancy Hoffman, Bob Schwartz, Lizbeth Schorr, Judy Codding, Mary Brabeck, Deborah Meier, Pedro Noguera, Sherry King, Van Schoales, Scott Hartl, Ron Rerger, Ron Wolk, Marie Ellen Larcada, Leslie Siskin, Courtney Ross, and two old friends who each supplied a deus ex machina—Ethan Lowenstein (thanks for the olive oil), and Eva Baker (thanks for the speech).

We also acknowledge the great advantage we have gained in our study by following paths created by earlier studies of going to scale in education. We owe much to Amanda Datnow, Lea Hubbard, and Hugh Mehan, who first called attention to the phenomenon of scaling up educational innovations in their 2001 book; and also to a number of Rand scholars, whose studies of New American schools and other reform initiatives have informed our thinking. They include Tom Glennan, Sue Bodilly, Mark Berends, Sheila Nataraj Kirby, Jolene Galgher, and Kerri Kerr.

Finally we thank the people who have supported us personally and professionally not only in the near decade of work that is reported here, but in years previous.

For Emily Klein, key supporters include Joe McDonald, whose scholarly work, creativity, and sense of narrative have served as a model for what it means to be an educational researcher, and Meg Riordan, who has been her partner in all research endeavors since the beginning. She also thanks Jerry Klein, whose passion for education has always been infectious and inspiring; Barbara Klein, who was her first, and best, teacher; and Tom Sugiura, husband and best friend, who has supported her growth as a teacher, writer, and researcher and makes it all worthwhile.

For Meg Riordan, these supporters include Joe McDonald, a thoughtful mentor who shepherded her toward opportunities for research and a career in experiential education; Emily Klein, thought-partner and friend who serves as an endless source of support; her family, whose belief and encouragement knows no bounds; and Andrew Campbell, who helps her to soar and somehow—magically—also manages to keep her grounded.

For Joe McDonald, key supporters include his research and writing partners, Emily Klein and Meg Riordan, who agreed to join in this somewhat crazy adventure. They also include Don Schön, who taught him the methods we used in this study; Ted Sizer, Pat Wasley and Rick Lear, who taught him the courage of reform; and Sarah Lawrence Lightfoot and David Cohen, who taught him how to write. Most especially, he thanks Beth McDonald, who vigilantly supports him in all things personal and professional, and Harry Gabor, the West Highland terrier who sat faithfully on nearby chairs as Joe worked on this book.

# 2

# The First Challenges

What we call the *first challenges* are not first because they can be dispatched early; indeed, all the challenges are recurring ones. They are first because school designers encounter them first and also because these challenges have an existential function to perform. They question what the design is. They also question how it can stay what it is, even as it evolves. And school designs *do* evolve. In this regard, they are more like software designs than fashion designs.

## THE FIRST CHALLENGES

1. *Fidelity Challenge.* Balancing fidelity and adaptation.
2. *Teaching Challenge.* Teaching and learning the design.
3. *Ownership Challenge.* Instilling shared ownership of the design.
4. *Communication Challenge.* Communicating effectively across contexts.
5. *Feedback Challenge.* Using experience in new settings to improve the design.

In this chapter we examine the first three of these challenges, saving the remaining two for the next chapter. In that chapter also, we consider all five by means of a distant mirror made of olive oil and other foodstuff. Throughout both chapters, we explore the strategies that BP evolved in order to address these first challenges. Below is a list of them. Each is useful in addressing more than one of the challenges.

## STRATEGIES FOR MANAGING THE FIRST CHALLENGES

1. *Articulation.* Laying out what the design stands for, what it consists of, and how it works.
2. *Differentiation.* Helping implementers understand what is compatible with the design and its underlying vision and what is not.

3. *Imagery*. Capturing the design in action for the benefit of those who need to understand it.
4. *Transparency*. Using visits to existing schools to guide design implementation elsewhere. Making design features, practices, and outcomes visible.
5. *Enculturation*. Engaging in symbolic shared experiences involving storytelling, ritual, and risk.
6. *Training*. Building expertise through explicit instructional protocols.

It is important to note that BP's replication strategies were not the product of research. There were no resources at BP to support such research. The New American Schools projects, including Expeditionary Learning Schools (ELS), did have the advantage of a brief period for pilot research in both design and strategic development. However, the Rand longitudinal study of their experience found that the projects continued to change substantially in design and strategy well beyond the pilot period, and indeed throughout the entire decade that Rand researchers studied them (Berends et al., 2002). If they were not the product of research, where did the BP strategies come from? We would say that they come especially from a process that Datnow, Hubbard, and Mehan (2001) call "the co-constructed nature" of going to scale with a whole-school design (p. 10). Co-construction by people we call school designers and people who implement their designs in the field is at the heart of all five of the first challenges (as well as the remaining three). It affects everything: the challenges, the strategies, and, of course, the design itself. We would also say that BP strategies have emerged from the intuition of BP staff members, as honed by their experience in diverse settings, and by the habitual practice at BP of pondering analogies beyond education (which we mimic in our use of distant mirrors).

## FIDELITY CHALLENGE: BALANCING FIDELITY AND ADAPTATION

Ignore fidelity and what will you take to scale? Ignore adaptation and your design will crack. This is more than just a challenge. It is a dilemma. It can only be managed, never resolved. The BP experience provided an especially good milieu in which to study the Fidelity Challenge because the BP design is so different from the conventional high school design, and difference accentuates demands for adaptation. At the same time, it is also simple, and simplicity accentuates demands for fidelity. Deborah Meier (2004) writes that BP schooling is based on "the oldest and most traditional idea around: Let kids learn mostly in the settings in which real people do interesting work" (p. vii). *Let's just try it clean and simple,* her words suggest. The complication is that turning school into what may seem to be not-school is threatening to many people—who include policymakers, teachers, parents, and kids themselves—even while it is inviting to many others in the same categories. So the other idea arises: *Maybe we better do the design differently here to avoid alienating some people.*

Such political calculation is not the only pressure toward adaptation. A BP staff member helped us understand the Fidelity Challenge by referring to jazz: "How do you keep jazz *jazz* and allow for growth? How do you honor forms, instrumentation, style virtuosity, and the deep-down funk of the past, yet not inhibit or constrain the perspective of newer artists?" He might just as well have reversed the analogy to the same effect, as in, "How do you impress standards on something so soulful, so fluid in form, so improvisatory?"

The key to managing the Fidelity Challenge is to give due deference to both poles of the dilemma it enfolds. Instead of choosing between fidelity and adaptation, you try to maximize both. This happens naturally, says BP cofounder and codirector Elliot Washor, if the designers talk continually about the design among various configurations of people, especially those taking action and those coaching action (people deeply cognizant of the context, and people deeply cognizant of the design). Such conversation involves the interplay of two strategies. In the first, which we call the *articulation strategy*, the school designer emphasizes fidelity and works to discover and then articulate the design's core principles, elements, and practices. In the second, which we call the *differentiation strategy*, the designer decides which of these principles, elements, and practices—if any— are inviolable and which can be adapted to suit particular contexts. This happens through the process of critically examining particular adaptations, then, as one BP staffer told us, giving or withholding a "nod of 'cool.'" A nod of cool honors the adaptation pole of the dilemma. It acknowledges that adaptation is needed, and that this one is "cool." At the same time, it implicitly honors the fidelity pole also. The very need to have such a review signifies that fidelity matters a lot—that it's possible to have a *bad* innovation. The differentiation strategy is thus an example of what BP cofounder and coleader Elliot Washor calls "and/both thinking." He refers to Jim Collins and Jerry Porras's (1994) admonition in *Built to Last* to reconcile what seem extreme contraries. Howard Wollner speaks below about the influence of this same text on Starbucks.

Articulation is fundamental to design of any kind. Other BP cofounder and coleader Dennis Littky illustrates this phenomenon with a reference to the work of the performance artists collectively known as Blue Man Group. Their art combines latex face masks painted with thick blue greasepaint, intense lighting, black clothing, large amounts of paper, muteness, social satire, drumming on oddly configured PVC piping, throwing food, and splattering paint. Blue Man began in an Off-Off Broadway theater in the East Village. Now it has several touring companies and more or less permanent performance venues not only in the East Village, but also in such places as Las Vegas; Berlin; Amsterdam; and Orlando, Florida. On the fidelity side, the Blue Men (and occasionally women) are guided by a 132-page operating manual. This is the thing that makes blue blue. It is the product of the three founding artists' efforts after a thousand New York performances to articulate what had by then become deeply held mutual understanding. Writing it down, says Rob Walker, not only took Blue Man deeper but gave it "transportability" (Walker, undated, online). It became performable by other artists willing to spend an hour getting into costume and willing also to follow the blue manual. In speaking to Walker about this milestone in the development of Blue Man Group, one of its founders, Matt Goldman, cites Francis Ford Coppola on the difference between making a good movie and a bad one: "getting everyone to make the *same* movie" (Walker, online). He thus perfectly evokes the fidelity pole of the dilemma. But fidelity is never enough. To stay fresh for multiple audiences and contexts, Blue Man Group must revise its work continually. The Village and Vegas, not to mention Berlin and Orlando, *are* different. "With each new project," writes Walker, "they confront the same decisions they've faced since the beginning. As Wink [Chris Wink, another of the three founding Blue Men] says, 'We're gonna have to go through each idea and say, Okay, that's all good and well, that's a nice thought—but is it Blue Man?' "(Walker, online). Our dialogue partner, Greg Farrell, says that he asks continually a similar question (though with a more ominous ring because of the Expeditionary Learning Schools [ELS] tendency to tolerate greater adaptation): "Is it a creative adaptation or a fatal mutation?"

Like Blue Man Group, BP was well established before it articulated its core elements—or what it came to call its "distinguishers"—those features that not only mark BP as BP but also in their absence indicate not-BP. These include advisory, Learning Through Internship (LTIs), learning plans, exhibitions, and family engagement. They form the basic topics for what BP calls "distinguishability talk." In distinguishability talk, BP tries to get clearer about what it means by advisory, for example, about its essence, about the boundaries of permissible adaptation. One of its champions within BP told us that the purpose of distinguishability talk "is not to gain control, but to raise questions about direction. If we keep doing this, where will it lead?" And how does where it will lead square with BP ideas?

Nor is the purpose of distinguishability talk to fix the point between fidelity and adaptation for all instances and circumstances—an effort that would likely threaten the disturbances or perturbations that Margaret Wheatley (1992) argues are the sources of continuing innovation. Thus an effort to handle one challenge too tightly—attempting to resolve rather than *manage* the dilemma of fidelity and adaptation—would risk intensifying another challenge on our list, the Feedback Challenge, about learning from experience. By the same token, successfully managing the Fidelity Challenge helps with the Feedback Challenge. If you develop a sense that it is possible under most circumstances to maximize both fidelity (to core ideas and practices) *and* adaptation (to contextual imperatives), you let down your guard to learning from experience. You know that learning from experience does not always threaten core ideas and practices. In the process you become more open to it even when it does, when it involves what Argyris and Schön (1978) call "double-loop learning," learning that does not just lead to corrections (single loop), but to rethinking fundamental orientations. In his 1997 book, Starbucks CEO Howard Schultz talks about his ban on serving lattes with nonfat milk, one of a long list of things that he initially said Starbucks would never do in its pursuit of the Americanized Milano espresso bar. The ban fell in the face of customer demand. Fidelity, Schultz decided in the end, rested on serving authentic coffee, not on interfering with customers' inclinations about what to mix with it.

Managing the Fidelity Challenge well also helps with the Ownership Challenge, number 3 on our list: instilling shared ownership of the design. In organizations like BP that begin in the creative intuition of one or two founders, a way must be found to spread intuition. Otherwise, scale that goes beyond a handful of sites overwhelms the organization's capacity to coach the emergence of authentic practice. Everyone remains dependent on the founders' opportunity to visit and personally approve or disapprove some local innovation. Distinguishability talk hones intuitive competence, and as a beneficial side effect, it grows ownership.

Our dialogue partner Howard Wollner tells us that the question of whether you can get a nonfat latte was just one of very many manifestations of the Fidelity Challenge that Starbucks wrestled with as it tried to turn Schultz's Milano coffee bar epiphany into coffee shops with "warm and inviting" store designs and trained baristas. As with BP, Wollner recalls, "the growth began organically with little documentation and lots of innovation. Intuition guided decisions and ideas flowed freely and frequently from all parts of the business, with the steady vision and drive of the founder acting as the 'true north.'" Here, too, Collins and Porras's reconstruction of *and* proved influential, as Wollner puts it:

> The management team at Starbucks embraced "the genius of the *and*" and ran with it. So often, we'd advance a business model, and

people would say, "You can't do that, it doesn't work that way." We'd say, "Well, we just did, and it does work." The point is that Starbucks didn't allow conventional wisdom to confine its thinking about the business and its possibilities. Each new store and each new market was a bit of an experiment. Could we open multiple stores? Could we open in more than one market? Could we open in markets far away from the original market? The answers we got as we asked these questions emboldened us because they were nearly always *yes*.

As Schultz (1997) puts it, "First, every company must stand for something. Starbucks stood not only for good coffee, but specifically for the dark-roasted flavor profile that the founders were passionate about. That's what differentiated and made it authentic" (p. 35). Wollner adds that what evolved from this authentic difference was a mission statement and guiding principles first articulated in 1990. Then from value-guided practice emerged a "culture that permeated everything that happened at the company. It was intuitive and ingrained in the people who worked at Starbucks," though it left room for regional differences too: "a beignet in New Orleans or a bagel in New York." Starbucks has never franchised its operations, though it eventually entered into licensing arrangements with grocery stores, airport concessionaires, and certain exclusive real estate venues. For the most part, however, it owns its outlets, and thus retains far more control than if it had franchised. It is the kind of control, as Wollner points out, that goes beyond consistency of design and can foster the evolution in each place of a strong culture, one that not only stays faithful to core principles but also encourages innovation. "Many of the best ideas came directly from partners (employees) at the store level who experimented with beverage ideas, for example, mixing what became the wildly popular Frappuccino."

In reading about the Fidelity Challenge as we have framed it, our other dialogue partner, Greg Farrell, says that it is good to have a name for a paradox that ELS has long lived with. However, he says he thinks of it less as a fidelity issue than as an infidelity issue—a matter of figuring out "where the tolerances are" for ELS as it goes about the task it has set for itself of stimulating teacher creativity. Here is how he puts it:

One part of our approach is to tap into teachers' passions and get them to imagine and create, and then support them in the creative act. This is part of our general strategy to treat teachers as professionals. They need to believe in their own academic capacity— working together or with a little help. We have the idea that we're trying to get teachers on a quest, and if they go on this quest, they're more likely to get students to go on one too. They don't have a prayer of getting students to be on a quest unless they're on one themselves.

## TEACHING CHALLENGE: TEACHING AND LEARNING THE DESIGN

This next challenge takes as a given that some people know the design well and can articulate it and differentiate its features from similar features in other designs. It also takes as a given that these people work with the design, maybe at the home office, maybe in a prototype school. The first part of this two-part challenge involves turning these people into design teachers, not just design workers. This part is the same old challenge we face whenever we become teachers of anything we know. We have to figure out how to admit other people to the intimacy of our knowing, how to follow their emerging sense of the object of knowledge, how to use this as a bridge to their understanding and their use of what they understand. You can teach a school design in different ways, and we highlight two of them below. However, it is important to note here that teaching it well ultimately requires having some people on hand who are expert teachers of the design. These are people (1) who deeply know the design in concept and practice, (2) who can empathize with other adults who need to know it, and (3) who know—whether by intuition or training—how to press for understanding without trying to force it. BP calls such people coaches.

We talk more about coaching in discussing another challenge on our list, the Communication Challenge. Here we'll simply say that one aspect of the Teaching Challenge is to help prospective coaches of the design learn as much about the design as the original designers know. Another aspect involves coming to terms with what it means to learn—*really* learn in the sense of giving up some other thing that is lodged in your brain in the same place where this new thing must go, *really* learn in the sense of being able to put the learning to use. When the object of knowledge is a school design, there are generally many people who need to become learners, not only coaches, but also principals, teachers, parents, students, policy actors at state and district levels, potential funders, union officials, employers, college admissions officers, journalists, and more.

The Teaching Challenge is an especially demanding one for BP because the BP design implicitly requires a significant degree of *un*learning, for example, concerning the nature of subject matter and of teaching expertise. The BP curriculum eschews traditional subject matter boundaries, and also the traditional idea of the classroom and the classroom teacher. BP schools are organized around advisories and Learning Through Internships (LTIs). BP knows that in teaching its design it has to find ways to help others imagine a kind of high schooling at odds with their own experience, and it expressly deals with unlearning as part of its coaching and training protocols.

Meanwhile, advisors also need personal and professional skills that classroom teachers do not necessarily need, skills associated, for example, with the negotiation of learning plans; the convening of advisees, parents, and mentors to develop such plans and to review progress in meeting them; the coaching of extended project work and of exhibition development; the one-on-one counseling of students; the investigation of learning opportunities and the coaching of learning at LTI sites about matters the advisor knows little about. And the LTI mentors need skills that photographers, landscapers, computer technicians, publicists, veterinarians, and so on do not usually need, skills associated, for example, with making your work transparent and articulating why you take the actions you take in particular circumstances.

The strategies that work so well for the Fidelity Challenge—articulating and differentiating—are insufficient for the Teaching Challenge. By themselves they seem to reduce teaching to telling and associate learning with the kind of discriminating tasks found on standardized tests. The other strategies on our list enrich the picture. Here we look at two of them: the *imagery strategy*, and the *transparency strategy*.

So the teachers of the design create images of it that are meant to draw the attention of learners to some of its key facets, thus teaching without telling. Perhaps the most instructive images of BP schooling, for example, are those from a series of photos by Cally Wolk of the hands and faces of BP school students as they interact with their mentors and others in workplaces. They suggest that this is a kind of schooling that involves being among adults doing real work in the world, and that the work is physical as well as mental. The latter is an important draw for many students, and for their parents, who sense what the students need and want in school. In their 2006 exploration of schools within schools, many of them vacuously "themed"—"the school of art and communication," "the school of international/cooperative learning," and so on—researchers Valerie Lee and Doug Ready encountered a number of students who had chosen a particular theme because it suggested to them (usually falsely) that it would at last be a school that would let them use their hands in learning. Under the influence especially of Elliot Washor, BP schools encourage minds-on learning that is also hands-on. And BP as an organization tries to capture this crucial nuance of its design in visual images. It is hard to imagine

BP headquarters without the photos that fill its walls of kids learning from mentors one-on-one and working with their hands. It is hard to imagine a BP event without a visually rich encounter, whether through a video or live show. BP calls its annual meeting the Big Bang, and these meetings are always rife with imagery. Big Bang VI, for example, in August 2007, opened with a brief articulation by Washor of the need "to lead with the hands" in BP teaching and learning, followed by an hour-long show by magician Mark Mitton, who happens also to be featured in Frank Wilson's 1998 book, *The Hand*. Mitton's bio, included in the Big Bang conference packet, says that "Mark is particularly interested in a concept of perception that includes both what we know and don't know, and finding a new way to accept our rational and irrational ways of looking at the world." Unlike most magic shows, his show, in the context of the BP focus on the hands and also its occasional "stop making sense" view of education in general, was not just highly entertaining, but also explicitly instructional.

Of course, people may first encounter BP schooling through verbal rather than visual images. Their sources may be the stories that BP students tell at recruitment events for new students, or at school board meetings where they testify as experts on the design. Or the stories may come from Dennis Littky's 2004 book about BP ideas, or Eliot Levine's 2002 book about the Met. Much of this verbal imagery seeks to capture another crucial nuance of the design, namely, its trust in the educational power of maturation. BP schools put kids—"one kid at a time" as the organization likes to say—in contexts that encourage the kids to emulate grown-ups, and then the schools wait more patiently than most schools do for the kids to grow up too. Many BP stories come down to the fact that BP kids *do* grow up.

An example of the role of transparency in teaching the design is the guided tour of BP schools, especially those on the Public Street campus in Providence. These four schools host more than 1,000 visitors a year. Here the shapes and functions of their rooms, the movable walls and unusual furniture, and the openness of the buildings to the poor neighborhood in which they are situated all serve to make the different curriculum seem feasible and its underlying ideas clearer and more compelling. In effect, they enable the prospective developer—the superintendent, the state or district official in charge of contracting vendors for new small schools, or the potential principal or funder—gain a new mental model about high schooling. The rooms at the Public Street campus even have descriptive placards, as if they were exhibits in a design show.

In another transparency effort, all BP schools are expected to produce weekly "TGIFs," collections of musings by voluntary contributors on their week's work, which are then shared across the network at Big Picture Online, the organization's intranet. Sometimes TGIFs are startling in their acknowledgment of difficulty or dissidence, and sometimes they seem to substitute personal for organizational transparency. But most often they are simply reflective accounts of the week's major events and cumulatively provide a rare account of the challenges and mundane realities of the enterprise overall.

BP schools gain transparency largely by encouraging openness and discouraging privacy among people who learn and teach in them. Visitors frequently visit advisories or stop individual students to talk about their work. Students are urged to think about these encounters as mutual opportunities in teaching and learning. They are the inside experts on the design, they are told, and they teach it to visitors. In so teaching, they obtain additional access to the adult world and additional perspectives on the interests that bring these outsiders to BP in Providence, Detroit, Camden, or Oakland. Meanwhile, students develop their learning plans with parents as well as their advisors, and the plans are shared with workplace mentors. Their exhibitions of progress are public, and the narratives of their progress are considered texts for discussion by a range of concerned adults—including advisors from other schools who may be brought in to participate in efforts to reorient students who have fallen behind in their progress toward graduation. Student work is frequently on display—not only in exhibitions, but in each school's daily "Pick Me Up," a morning all-school ritual that often features student performance, and in videos and print materials and wall hangings intended to articulate the school's values to its own community as well as outsiders. Advisors are expected to discuss their advisory work openly with their principals, and in turn the principals are expected to discuss their own work openly with Dennis Littky and Elliot Washor, and with BP coaches.

Reflecting on the use of transparency as a strategy for teaching the design, our dialogue partner Howard Wollner tells us about the creation of the Starbucks Support Center (the name involving an implicit rejection of the usual term *corporate headquarters*). The Support Center is located in a former Sears catalog distribution center within a light-industry area south of downtown Seattle. It was "a white elephant of a building," Wollner remembers (he being the one who found it and oversaw its renovation), "and in a part of the city not yet considered suitable for corporate offices." Each floor had more than 130,000 square feet, the equivalent of 6–7 stories of a typical high-rise. This was space that invited unorthodox design, all of it purposefully instructive, as Wollner describes:

> Executive offices were not placed on the perimeter of the building with the windows. They were placed inboard so that light could flow in and be shared and enjoyed by the largest number of people.

Investments were made in lots of casual lounges clustered around stairways connecting each floor where people could accidentally meet and hold impromptu discussions. Large functional groups were mixed by floors so that people with different responsibilities within the business would end up knowing each other and sharing their diverse perspectives and responsibilities for the business. Each of these decisions, while small, were intentional and suggested to people entering the environment that something different was happening in this space—a difference that people should carry forward in their thinking about the business in general.

## OWNERSHIP CHALLENGE: INSTILLING SHARED OWNERSHIP OF THE DESIGN

In *Bread and Butter: What a Bunch of Bakers Taught Me About Business and Happiness*, Tom McMakin (2001), former CEO of the Great Harvest Company, a franchising bakery, writes:

> On the one hand, we love quality. We are stubbornly opinionated about the best way to run a bread company. Taken by itself, this idea would lead to an autocratic operation committed to strict quality standards uniformly enforced on all franchisees. We have a second ideal, equally strong, however. We believe that no person, society, or institution can be great without liberty. In our hierarchy of values, freedom is at the top. (p. 51)

Great Harvest manages the Fidelity Challenge through a back-door approach that calls more attention to the Ownership Challenge. On the one hand, it seems to abandon fidelity nearly completely in what it calls the "freedom franchise." Although every owner must display the Great Harvest sign, purchase premium wheat from approved suppliers, and fresh-mill the flour, there are no rules regarding recipes or store design or product selection. In fact, the franchise contract states, "Anything not expressly prohibited by the language of this agreement is allowed" (McMakin, 2001, p. 52). However, the company takes steps to ensure that franchise owners do not manage their businesses in isolation. It wants them to feel like owners of Great Harvest, not just a Great Harvest franchise. In effect, Great Harvest tries to manage the Fidelity Challenge by focusing more on the Ownership Challenge and the Teaching Challenge. McMakin says that encouraging a "learning community" is central to the Great Harvest strategy (p. 60). Thus Great Harvest supports a "cross-travel program" in which an owner or employee of a bakery can visit another bakery. Great Harvest pays for half the cost of the travel—no reports, no permission, no questions (p. 63).

BP's success to date has hinged on its ability to instill a similarly metaphorical ownership among the people who lead BP schools, work in them, attend them, send their kids to them, and support them in other ways. These "owners" tend to become enthusiastic teachers of the design, testifying about it before school boards and other policymaking groups or talking about it on visits to BP schools or in videos.

In their study of the scaling up of the National Writing Project (NWP), McDonald, Buchanan, and Sterling (2004) claim that ownership in this broader and metaphorical sense rests ultimately on risk-taking. Writing and sharing writing—two activities that most people find risky—are central activities of every NWP workshop or conference. NWP thus forces teachers at every turn to face the same risks that their students will face if the teachers follow the project's tenets. Thus the teachers come to understand writing more deeply, namely, from the inside as writers themselves. In the process, the teachers also bond with each other (having undergone risk together) and end up bonding with the project too. Writing as risk-taking becomes for NWP what Elliot Washor calls the "glue" that holds the scaled-up operation together. Reacting to Washor's metaphor, our dialogue partner Greg Farrell tells us that in the foundation world where he once worked, people speak of "glue money," which he adds "is like 'walking-around money,'—what you need to get things going and get people going." Glue is for adherence, he suggests, which is fundamental to coherence.

While the *imagery strategy* and the *transparency strategy* are good at connecting people to the design, intriguing them with its properties, and familiarizing them with its details, strategies that press for a risk-taking plunge are necessary to instill ownership. Two are the *enculturation strategy* and the *training strategy*. The first envelops the learner within a community focused on the design, while the second guides him or her through protocols intended to teach serious design expertise. Both involve risk-taking. By means of the first, the learner puts aside misgivings and disbelief in order to try on ownership. By means of the second, the learner takes on the actual responsibilities of ownership.

All companies use some form of enculturation to adjust newcomers to their values and organizational norms. However, we use the term to mean something more intensive and more deeply cultural. In this sense it is associated with what organizational theorists Lee Bolman and Terry Deal (1997) call the symbolic frame. This is the frame within which organizations become "tribes, theaters, or carnivals," where learning is "propelled more by rituals, ceremonies, stories, heroes, and myths than by rules, policies, and managerial authority" (p. 14). BP's use of the strategy became most visible to us in August 2002 when we observed the extravaganza that launched the first BP schools outside Providence, a 3-day event called the Big Bang. The name has stuck to BP's annual network get-togethers. The first Big Bang included songs and new games; a "living time line" on which everyone present stood, including the real Ted Sizer and someone impersonating John Dewey (who handed out original-issue postal stamps with Dewey's image on them); moving personal testaments about struggle and diversity, by Met advisors and Met students; a "Pick Me Up" (the morning ritual in Big Picture schools) in the form of a game show; giant puppets who mingled with diners and pretended to mistake the Big Bang for a wedding reception; and a football kickoff that involved raining tiny footballs stamped "The Big Picture Company" (the event happened at the summer training camp of the New England Patriots). Participants who included principals and staff from all the new schools left the event bearing pictures of every other participant as well as a Big Picture T-shirt and a ribboned medal. An advisor in one of the new schools we visited later recalled the Big Bang fondly. "I don't think I could have bought the philosophy without being around the people," he said, though he added, "It almost felt like a cult." The last remark reveals the risk he felt. The *almost* in his sentence may be the result of the fact that the Big Bang also included serious workshops and conversations—in other words, training as well as enculturation.

Reflecting on our writing about the Big Bang by the light of his experience in Expeditionary Learning Schools (ELS), Greg Farrell acknowledges first of all the association of ELS with Outward Bound (OB). The latter practices what might be called a pedagogy of enculturation and is deeply committed to the idea that growth can come from opening yourself to risk. Indeed, "on OB courses," Farrell says, "we get some of the most revelatory commentary about learning—even when people are not themselves in the learning business. Someone might say, 'Now I understand how students feel when they fail.'" On the other hand, he adds, OB does not intuitively strike most people as related to school reform or reading and writing. "So prospective partners can write us off if we're not careful," he says. "'I'm not interested in camping,' they might say, 'I want these kids to read.'" To help them unlearn part of this association and accommodate a different one, ELS has invented an explicitly academic adventure, called a *summit* (the word evoking the adventure of a wilderness climb). Adults learn about ELS in an intense weeklong Learning Expedition where they are immersed as if they were students in particular content learning, for example, involving science, the arts, history, and complete with deep experiences in reading and writing. As in an OB course, Farrell says, "You don't stop and say, 'Now we're working on courage.' You just deal with courage, perseverance, compassion—or whatever—intentionally and explicitly, but also lightly." This explicitness—though on the side, so to speak—marks the boundary between enculturation and training.

As with the other strategies we are discussing in this chapter, enculturation requires a deft touch. It begins by enfolding newcomers into a culture as if the culture were already theirs. This is an especially effective move at the point just past first commitment, in the early stages of community building. This is when, as Grossman, Wineburg, and Woolworth (2001) put it, "individuals have a natural tendency to play community— to act as if they are already a community that shares values and common beliefs . . . to 'behave as if we all agree'" (p. 955). The play scaffolds learning the new culture's tenets and attitudes. Nonetheless, play is still play, and the community, as Grossman, Wineburg, and Woolworth put it, is merely a pseudocommunity. For it to become a real community, the newcomers must gain a voice, must find a way to bring their own work on its own terms into the cultural circle. And the training strategy is their ticket of admission. That is because training—at least as we use the term— implicitly acknowledges the capacity of the trainee to become as expert as the trainer. So it is not training as in "I trained the dog," but as in "I took my first training in the new surgical technique." This involves risk-taking too: actually daring to go deep, to become, in fact, the surgeon with the new surgical technique.

BP puts special emphasis on the training of principals, since it regards them as the linchpin leaders of its design. Their training occurs at weekend and summer events like the Big Bang and also accompanies their residencies at BP schools, though residencies are no longer standard practice because of the cost. BP training focuses on such diverse and specific skills as assessing the depth of student projects, fund-raising, building community relationships, and analyzing data. In the process, it aims for shared ownership, though less precipitously than the enculturation strategy. Yet, as we say, it involves at least as much risk-taking. On the short side of genuine expertise, it suggests, you can't really know what expertise means. You have to take the plunge first, risk destabilizing your ordinary sense of curriculum, leadership, and community connection in order to gain a different sense of these things. One BP coach we interviewed captured this for us in a reference he made to trainees' questions. He does not "criticize questioning," he said, particularly around how to "improve the quality of our work." He cautioned, however, against questioning the "viability" of the BP school design, calling instead for "faith" in it. Collins and Porras (1994) say that the companies they describe in *Built to Last* practice "indoctrination into a core ideology"—not just a core culture—and promote "a sense of belonging to something special and superior" (p. 123).

Our dialogue partner Howard Wollner reports the Starbucks experience in this regard:

> Whenever Starbucks opened a new Market—whether it was Dallas, Texas, or Spain—new partners who were hired to open the market were brought to the Starbucks Seattle Support Center and spent 12 weeks in intensive training, learning all aspects of the business from each key discipline. These new market partners included the head of the market, the first few new store managers, and often even baristas hired to work in the first stores that were to open. This was a huge investment of time and money for both the partner opening the new market and for the people working in the Starbucks Support Center who shared their knowledge of the Starbucks business. That said, it was probably the best investment that could possibly be made to ensure the success of the future market. The culture was set in place and allowed to flourish as these vanguard partners returned to their market to begin delivering the Starbucks Experience to new customers. In addition, an opening team of seasoned Starbucks partners would travel to the market and spend anywhere from 8 to 12 weeks working in the new market alongside the market partners—again to ensure consistency of the experience.

When Howard Schultz returned as CEO of Starbucks, after having been out of the role for 3 years, and in the wake of a 50% drop in the company's share price, one of his first recovery tactics was to close more than 7,000 U.S. stores for 3 hours of cross-company training focused on the importance of proper beverage preparation, customer connection, and store appearance. "A great theatrical stroke," David Margolick (2008) called it in a *Conde Nast Portfolio* article, but we would call it reculturation through retraining.

The training strategy hands over the keys, not permanently at first, but just for a test drive, just for the evening. Still, the person with the keys can drive wherever he or she chooses. Of course, the goal of the Ownership Challenge is *shared* ownership, so the keys metaphor has its limits; nevertheless, BP wants and needs to instill considerable ownership in the people who lead and work in local BP schools. It understands from experience that absent local ownership and the power it grants to "drive"—for example, to wrestle in an authoritative way with the challenge of balancing fidelity and adaptation—the design will dissolve in the politics of context. It understands also that absent local ownership, BP will lack the local teachers of the design who are needed to teach it again and again to other local people, including people who might otherwise try to stamp it out.

On the other hand, BP wants to ensure that all this ownership has a firm footing in the values that underlie the design.

The enculturation strategy implicitly asks newcomers to suspend any disbelief they might have so as to experience the values deeply, while the training strategy asks them to undergo a deskilling/reskilling transformation and in the process gain a voice in the application as well as the possible revision of BP values. Together, the strategies invite newcomers to "put skin in the game." That's what investors call it when leaders buy stock in their own company.

# 3

# Two More Challenges
# and a Distant Mirror

In this chapter we examine two more of what we call the *first* challenges. In the process, we add to the list of strategies outlined in Chapter 2.

### Two More Challenges

- *Communication Challenge.* Communicating effectively across contexts.
- *Feedback Challenge.* Using experience in new settings to improve the design.

### Two More Strategies for Managing the First Challenges

- *Coaching.* Assisting implementation through close observation and consultation. Conferring with local implementers about the adaptations they make and why.
- *Building and Networking Communities of Practice.* Encouraging the local exchange and networking of practical knowledge.

## COMMUNICATION CHALLENGE:
## COMMUNICATING EFFECTIVELY ACROSS CONTEXTS

Context number 1 is the home office. Context number 2 is the first set of schools—the prototype schools. Context number 3 is the next set of schools. That is when intimacy begins to become less constant and more periodic and when problem solving that asks home office staff to drop everything and pitch in to help becomes difficult. This is also the point in a scaling-up process when the home office begins to feel some strain, when, for example, the staff gets too big to make decisions collectively or begins to seem too generalist in its knowledge base. BP was just at this point when we began our study.

Yet organizational theorist Tom Peters (1987) had just told Dennis Littky that BP growth was still much too small even to be associated with the word *scale*. He said that it was still "play." What he meant was that BP still had time to keep figuring things out as it moved along—a method that tends to serve start-ups well in any field. This is because it produces lots of feedback fast. When an organization is willing to pay attention to this feedback, the result is good learning fast. And when the ratio of intimacy to distance (though changing) is still weighted toward intimacy, the process of attending to feedback needs no special communication infrastructure. *Being there* is a given. Later, however, *being there* takes much more effort, and this is when the communication challenge kicks in.

To manage the challenge, BP has used many of the strategies we discussed in the preceding chapter. It learned to articulate its design more thoroughly—first in big red binders, then in Web-based formats. It invented differentiation rituals like "distinguishability talk" and enculturation rituals like the Big Bang. It devised training regimens like "TYBO"—a residency for principals in The Year Before Opening. These strategies all serve to balance fidelity and adaptation, to teach the design, and to instill shared ownership, and they are implicitly communication vehicles too. Moreover, BP has other communication vehicles. Shortly after we began our study, it built an intranet that it uses to share training materials, curriculum documents, and student work; to support email and encourage list-based conversations; and to manage synchronous and asynchronous forums. A little later it invested in video conferencing, including one set of video conferences based on what Elliot Washor called a reality TV series about the life of an advisory in one BP school. Such vehicles have communicated core values to new schools as well as to new staff and have fed back information to all staff about the new contexts in which BP operates.

Beyond these, BP also uses one other strategy to address the Communication Challenge that we want to highlight. This is the *coaching strategy*. Use of the word *coaching* is ubiquitous today among people involved in school designing and school reform generally. It typically denotes the teaching activities of a set of people deeply knowledgeable about a particular curriculum or school design and skillful in helping others learn it. In this sense, as we mentioned in the previous chapter, coaching is a crucial strategy in addressing the teaching challenge. Dennis Littky helped us understand, however, that coaching is also a crucial form of communication. Here is how he put it in interview remarks that are deeper than the transcription alone can convey, and that we analyze below:

You should probably do a section on all the things that went wrong. Because people don't know. People think, ah, it looks so smooth. That's why I call this stuff magic. What makes something magic is that you don't see the stuff in between—you know, sleight of hand [at this point in the interview, he makes a card disappear from several he shuffles]. One of the reasons people have trouble scaling up is that people don't talk about their flaws. So, 2 years, and the principal you trained is gone. So you have to work that. If you don't work that right, if you're not in at the right time, all of a sudden you get the assistant principal from the high school who moves in, and your school is gone. It's about knowing that, being there enough, and then staying there and doing it. There are all these things that no one sees. So somehow people have to know all that, and that that's OK, that it's about going through a lot, and still going out there.

Reading this bit of transcript, our dialogue partner Greg Farrell had a strong reaction: "He's got it. He understands this work very well—sizing up the local politics, learning which way to go, who to go with, taking the time to learn the culture, make the connections. And, then making the right moves at the right times whether they have to do with resources or fidelity." Meanwhile, we had done a close reading of Littky's comments. We wanted to know what exactly Littky meant by such phrases as "going out there," being "in at the right time," "staying there," "being there enough," and "you have to work that." We wondered especially about his saying, "Somehow people have to know all that . . . that it's about going through a lot, and still going out there." We examined the interview transcript by the light of other data we had gathered, particularly with regard to Littky's concern at the time that BP had overcommitted to the Bill and Melinda Gates Foundation and as a result was building too many schools too fast. And we decided that Littky's *there,* as in "going out *there,*" and "being *there* enough," and "still going out *there,*" is wherever design meets a new—and to the designer's eye, strange—context, beyond the first ring of context, when intimacy is still a given. *There* is where the potential exists that the design will disintegrate upon contact with some unknown and un*worked* element of the strange context. BP needs to be "in at the right time" to "work it." This is the *coaching strategy.* And the "sleight of hand" Littky was asking us to investigate, understand, and ultimately reveal has to do with communication.

When you think about it, communication almost always involves sleight of hand, for example, the mysterious and hidden processes by which Google answers my question, or my text message reaches someone else's eyes, or a conference gets onto my iPod. Mostly this "magic," as Littky called it, is not evident to us, unless someone else's surprise illuminates it. For example, a preschooler once asked a principal we know whether she was the lady whose voice was in the wall. The child was referring to morning announcements. And a 90-year-old asked one of us once how something as big as the Internet could fit into something as small as a Blackberry. In our interview, Littky was shrewdly playing the part of the preschooler and the nonagenarian.

When you think about coaching as a communication strategy—rather than merely as a strategy for teaching the design—you highlight its interpretive dimension. Coaches are essentially boundary spanners. They work at the intersection of institutions. On the one hand, there is the school design home office, and on the other, there are the schools that have adopted the design. Coaches "go out there," as Littky put it—far out on a limb, he might have added. A recent book about boundary spanning edited by Howey and Zimpher (2006) documents the risks implicit in such work. They include feeling something of a stranger in both institutions, somewhat isolated and even endangered professionally. They also include nearly always operating in highly ambiguous circumstances and with generally dubious license. But the book suggests that the benefits justify the risks. The authors of one chapter in the Howey and Zimpher book say that boundary spanners create and manage "physical and philosophical safe spaces and opportunities between and among the collaborating constituencies" (Clark, Foster, & Mantle-Bromley, 2006, p. 35). These are the spaces within which deep communication can occur and where the right balance between fidelity and adaptation can be determined. On the one hand, the boundary-spanning coaches are accountable for the vision. On the other hand, they are the sensors for the demands of context. Perched smack on top of the Fidelity Challenge, they carry messages in both directions: to encourage fidelity *and* adaptation. Francine Peterman, in the same 2006 volume, associates this communicative/coaching/boundary spanning with Seymour Sarason's (1972) famous phrase "the creation of future settings." The "settings" are the schools themselves—the product ultimately of successful communication between design and context. Boundary spanners facilitate all this by a sleight of hand that leads without seeming to, that promotes the design and its underlying vision without hardballing, that carries back the feel of contextual demands without seeming to encourage what BP disparagingly calls "backsliding," and that quietly and continuously calculates the ratio of risk to advantage in particular adaptations.

Greg Farrell says that all this is why Expeditionary Learning Schools calls its school coaches "school designers." This is the right term, he thinks, because these are the people who create "practical coherence" where it matters most, who bring knowledge closest to action. They help principals and teachers, as Farrell puts it, "set one thing right in order to enable other things to be right." And over the course of 15 years, the ELS school designers have learned to do this in a rigorous way, as he explains:

> Using a Core Practice Benchmark book—a set of benchmarks against which we annually review the level of implementation of every school, a school designer in New York or another place will make observations of a school she's working with. Over time—and this is meant to be a process rather than an event—she will gather information on how each teacher is teaching. Then with the school's leadership team and principal, she will assess how the school is doing on Core Practices—Active Pedagogy, Learning Expeditions, Culture/Character and the others—and arrive at a discussed rating. There are 16 indicators, with the bulk focused on instruction, especially Learning Expeditions and Active Pedagogy.

Starbucks doesn't have coaches, but it has Support Center partners who play a similar role. Howard Wollner tells us that on their visits to stores in the field, both the Support Center partners and the store partners learn a lot. "There is no good substitute for a personal dialogue between people with differing responsibilities and perspectives," he adds, "and as organizations grow, so does their need to create more such contact points." He argues that such contact points protect the home office from rigidity and presumptuousness in terms of who has the most important knowledge. Here is how he puts it:

> The challenge is to create processes, but to avoid bureaucracy. Starbucks always walked a fine line in this regard. For example, all stores must understand the latest promotion and set up the same way and at the same time. However, as seasoned managers would often say, they learned to discern from all the information that was being sent out on a weekly basis what they needed to pay attention to and what information just got in the way. This process of discernment became the hallmark of effective and successful store managers. The lesson here for the home office is to pare down communication and only deliver essential information, avoiding the temptation to overcommunicate. It is always better to have the field wanting more support and asking questions than to overcommunicate and find that some people in the field eventually throw up their hands in frustration. The key to staying nimble and

innovative is to standardize those aspects of the business that require consistency and create the greatest efficiency, while allowing decisions to be made closest to the customer.

It may be useful to think of coaches as jump-drive communicators. They bring all the design knowledge "out there," as Littky would say, as if the knowledge were on the jump drive at the end of their key chains. And what they do out there is work on the creation of "practical coherence," as Farrell puts it, drawing on the design knowledge as needed. In the process, they protect the design knowledge from home office communication crashes, or as Wollner puts it, "overcommunication." Under the pressures of scaling up, home offices themselves can crash and, in the process, seriously threaten design knowledge. Over the course of our three-year study of BP's replication efforts, BP nearly completely turned over its home staff, not once but twice, not least because it needed experts in the various communication strategies it pursued. However, its coaching staff, including Littky and Washor, remained fairly stable.

## FEEDBACK CHALLENGE: USING EXPERIENCE IN NEW SETTINGS TO IMPROVE THE DESIGN

This challenge is at the heart of what it means to be a learning organization. That's Peter Senge's (1990) term for an organization designed for continuous adaptation and improvement. Again, nearly all the strategies we've discussed above can help address this challenge, from *differentiation*, which clarifies experience in new settings, to *coaching*, which communicates the subtleties of experience in new settings. However, the eighth strategy on our list is necessary in the end to meet the challenge fully. This is the strategy of *building and networking communities of practice*. Communities of practice and networks of practice are the brains of successful design replication.

Communities of practice are still rare in American schooling. In their 1999 study of mathematics teaching in Germany, the United States, and Japan, Stigler and Hiebert (1999) observe that U.S. teachers mostly work alone. Their book calls attention to the pernicious impact of this on the knowledge base for teaching. Each retirement means a loss of memory. Other studies have lamented the impact on accountability. For example, Carnoy, Elmore, and Siskin (2003) conclude that external demands for accountability often fail for want of an internal capacity to respond effectively to them and to organize for the professional learning they require. When it comes to schooling by design, we think that teacher isolation is the ultimate blockade. In order to scale up, school designers must address it. Most address it by trying to build local communities of practice, and also by trying to network the locals.

The term *community of practice* was coined by Jean Lave and Etienne Wenger (1991). They used it to describe the rich and complex social environments that enveloped the apprenticeships they studied. It turns out that most apprenticeships introduce the apprentice not just to the mentor's practice but to the mentor's world of practice. The result, Lave and Wenger conclude, is situated learning, a concept that proved influential in the development of contemporary learning theory (Bransford, Brown, & Cocking, 2000). Indeed, the concept of situated learning underlies and justifies the BP design's heavy reliance on internships, what they call Learning Through Internships or LTIs.

In 1995, John Seeley Brown, the longtime chief scientist at the Xerox Corporation, and Estee Solomon Gray (1995) adopted the term *community of practice* to refer to a strategy for creating and managing knowledge in commercial settings. Their classic *Fast Company* article, "The People Are the Company," tells the story of how a group of anthropologists in the 1980s shadowed a bunch of Xerox copier repair technicians as the latter went about their work. The anthropologists' findings "challenged the way Xerox thought about the nature of work, the role of the individual, and the relationship between the individual and the company" (p. 78). The repair technicians learned more about how to repair machines by swapping stories with one another informally than by consulting repair manuals, and thus what appeared to the company to be downtime in terms of their productivity—when, for example, the technicians were hanging out together at the coffee pot in the local parts warehouse—was actually *up* time. "The tech reps weren't slacking off: they were doing some of their most valuable work . . . co-producing insights about how to repair machines better" (p. 78). Here is how Brown and Gray (1995) describe communities of practice in this context:

> At the simplest level, they are a small group of people who've worked together over a period of time. Not a team, not a task force, not necessarily an authorized or identified group. People in CoPs [Communities of Practice] can perform the same job (tech reps) or collaborate on a shared task (software developers) or work together on a product (engineers, marketers, and manufacturing specialists). They are peers in the execution of "real work." What holds them together is a common sense of purpose and a real need to know what each other knows. There are many communities of practice within a single company, and most people belong to more than one of them. (p. 81)

Having learned about the communities of practice lurking within it, Xerox set out to systematize the phenomenon. For example, it tried to add additional learning power through technology, giving technicians two-way radios so they could consult with each other on the job in real time. Later, Xerox also introduced one of the first Web-based environments for swapping stories of practice, in effect seeking to network the local communities of practice.

Today, many organizations in many fields, including the field of schooling by design, regard workplace teams and the relationships they form in real time and virtual time as crucial substructures of the organizations overall. This is where they expect much learning from experience to occur, and the smartest innovations to originate. Many of these organizations are also cognizant of the potential power of networking these communities—or of creating what are sometimes called networks of practice—in order to use experience in myriad settings to improve designs and designing.

Education researchers have tended to apply the concept of "community of practice" to the formal as well as the informal sphere. This is not surprising given the severely cellular design of traditional schooling, where individual teachers typically work alone in the basic organizational element called a classroom. Nearly any formal departure from the cellular can seem as remarkable in schooling as the informal communities of practice seemed at Xerox. Fred Newmann and Gary Wehlage (1995), reporting on a national study of restructured schools, claimed that the most successful of these schools "were the ones that used restructuring tools to help them function as professional communities of practice" (p. 3). They formed planning teams, they taught together, they evaluated student work together. Where such communities enjoyed the right supports and focused on students' intellectual growth, the researchers reported, students did grow intellectually. In a study of high schools, McLaughlin and Talbert (2001) found a subsample of schools that proved consistently able to get and keep a diverse group of students academically engaged. A key marker of these schools was the presence of a "strong professional community committed to making innovations that support student and teacher learning and success" (pp. 38–39). In a 2006 book, McLaughlin and Talbert account for what such communities do: "They build and manage knowledge; they create shared language and standards for practice and student outcomes; and they sustain aspects of their school's culture vital to continued, consistent norms and instructional practice" (p. 5).

These are crucial activities to undertake in a school seeking to learn and implement a design. When they happen across many local contexts, and are coached by people working to understand and communicate insights and innovations that may improve the design, they become the principal strategy for meeting the Feedback Challenge.

What does it take to build a community of practice in a school? The first requirement is leadership. In all the instances where they found strong communities of practice, McLaughlin and Talbert also found a leader explicitly focused on developing and sustaining the community. Sometimes the leader came from within the school, and sometimes he or she was an outside coach. Their finding about the importance of such leadership dovetails with a finding by Wenger, McDermott, and Snyder (2002), who studied communities of practice in business. Such leaders organize the work of the community of practice—offering it focus and purpose, tending its norms, managing its interface with more formal governance. They also massage its learning environment through a facilitation that fosters both urgency and respect (McDonald, Mohr, Dichter, & McDonald, 2007; McLaughlin & Talbert, 2006). Wenger's (1998) advice about communities of practice in general suggests what else is necessary beyond leadership. Communities of practice also require a *shared domain of interest*, for example, an interest in making a school design work in a particular context; *joint activities*, for example, studying student work together; and *relationship*, for example, feeling the bonds of shared ownership of the design.

Early in our BP study, two Met advisors we interviewed gave us good examples of the kind of knowledge that gets passed around a community of practice once it is established. One example has to do with the predictable rhythm of advising in a BP school:

> Right about week 6 of an advisory, there's a thing that happens: Kids aren't really getting it, and at the same time they are getting over the glow of being in a place where they are known, have personal freedoms unknown in their middle school experience, et cetera. But they're not getting it with respect to out-of-the-box thinking, real-world learning, passion. You can only suspend disbelief for so long, however good the place feels, then a frenzy hits: "What am I learning? Nothing." That's when the advisor has to kick it up.

Another example illuminates what it mean to advise in a supportive and also pragmatic way:

> A kid in your advisory says he wants to build a whole new wing of the United Nations. What do you do? Put the kabbosh on it and risk dampening the passion that underlies the idea? Or, say the kid says she wants to study dolphins for her LTI. The advisor thinks, "Whoa, that's not going to lead to real-world learning, because we live in a landlocked place." Do you say it? No, you work to hone it down,

and at the same time preserve its essential character. "You have good ideas," the advisor needs to learn to say, "now let's get the details right."

We asked how these advisors learned these things about advising. "From 4 years of screwing up," one answered quickly, then added that he had learned them also over those years by hanging around the Trinity Brew House on Fridays after work, swapping stories with other advisors. The Trinity Brew House is a pub near the original Met campus. "Screwing up"—which is to say, experimenting continually on the job—plus telling stories with coworkers about the experiments in an informal setting, equal the Brown and Gray definition of a community of practice.

When we met them, these two advisors had just become coaches. One later became the head of BP coaching, overseeing the work of several regional coaches. How do advisors-turned-coaches spread what they learned at work (and after work) in Providence or elsewhere to people working at other schools in other places? How do they make what remains still relatively tacit knowledge public knowledge? How do they connect one community of practice with another? This is the second part of the toughest strategy on our list of strategies: building *and* networking communities of practice. It is critical to meeting the feedback challenge.

Our dialogue partner Greg Farrell suggests that communities of practice in the domain of schooling by design are constructed from the beginning across the boundaries that ordinarily insulate schools. Thus the first schools that ELS worked with in creating the ELS design became partners in the design. The trick of networking communities of practice, he thinks, is to build on this beginning, to ensure that the partnering continues through coaches or the ELS school designers who extend it to their colleagues and to all the schools in the network. He thinks that the ELS principle derived from Kurt Hahn through Outward Bound of "crew, not passengers" helps in this regard. It makes partnering mandatory—nobody gets to sit back. A consequence, he says, is that "we're still learning a lot from our schools—and in the process innovating in ways we would not otherwise have." He recalls having lunch recently with the principal of a new ELS school in Oakland, California. When Farrell marveled over the qualities of teaching and learning he had just observed in the school, the principal seemed surprised. "But you're the founder," he said. "You're the person whose idea this was!" Farrell responded, "My idea wasn't this good!"

Early into BP's scaling-up efforts, Elliot Washor mused for us on the Feedback Challenge and offered a metaphor for networking communities of practice:

I was sitting on the plane yesterday, and I was thinking of 44
schools in another 3 to 5 years, and it takes another 3 to 5 years for
them to reach capacity—so we're really talking 5 to 10 years for
these 44 schools. I said to myself, "Well, I can get around to a
dozen, but I don't know how good I'm going to be at getting around
to 44." So then what does it mean? I think a bunch of people are
going to have to do that to keep the glue going.

The "bunch of people" who he says are needed to network the BP
communities of practice are the coaches that BP was then beginning to use.
His anxiety here is partly about whether it can produce the right coaches,
but it is also about what the coaches can do. Most existing corporate networks of practice rely on sophisticated networking technology that aims
to make the technology as nearly invisible and unobtrusive as possible,
though they rely also on face-to-face connectors (Hildreth & Kimble, 2004).
Valdis Krebs, an international management consultant who has worked
with many large corporate clients, develops sophisticated software to map
social networks existing within the corporations. He calls the maps "organizational X-rays" (McGregor, 2005). To assist his clients, he uses the maps
to locate people operating near the borders of adjacent networks and then
to introduce them and create opportunities for them to work together. Over
time, he says, people learn to trust one another, and the overall organization thereby gains greater coherence, also known as *glue*.

Greg Farrell says that he thinks ELS has actually made greater progress
in networking its communities of practice because it is more people dependent than technology dependent. "That's why the hugging at the
national conference. They met before and have been through something
together." He adds, "I know that the world is moving in the way of virtual
communication, but for the kinds of things we want to communicate it's not
good enough. I'm reluctant to turn it all over to technology. You know, you
can't take an Outward Bound course except by being there." To facilitate face-
to-face connection, ELS has pursued a clustered approach in going to scale.
Farrell enumerates some of the clusters: "We have 7 schools in New York
City, and we'll have 10–12 in the next few years. Colorado has 14 or 15. Our
biggest cluster is in the Northwest, with quite a collection in Oregon. We
have a cluster in the Bay Area and strong ones in New England." Asked how
these clusters developed, Farrell says that "much of it is talent dependent—
for example, the influence of ELS staff members Scott Hartl and Ron Berger."
And some is resource dependent: "We also have a big cluster in Kansas City
because of a good relationship with the Kaufmann Foundation there."

Reflecting on the Starbucks experience in dealing with the Feedback
Challenge amid its vast and worldwide scaling-up, our dialogue partner

Howard Wollner notes, by contrast, the crucial role that technology has played. "When Starbucks reached a critical mass with its international business," he says, "we had to find a way to allow best practices to reach and take root in a far-flung system—stores that are open somewhere in the world at every hour of the day and night." The Starbucks intranet became the communication platform. It was a 2-year process, Wollner says, "to create a global business system that would take the tribal knowledge of all the partners who had expertise and capture it in a searchable way. For example, he continues, "there may have been successful marketing campaigns, say, in Taiwan and Greece, and Mexico and Australia could see what had been done and use that work as a starting point for creating their own campaign." This communication challenge was always interlaced, Wollner reports, with the Fidelity Challenge: "The fine line that had to be walked was to allow for autonomy and appropriate adaptation, while protecting the essence of the brand."

Like Greg Farrell, however, Wollner also emphasizes the role of people engaging face to face, too, and mentions the qualities they need to network productively: "strong people skills, including listening to and sharing information about what works and, most importantly, what doesn't work so valuable time isn't spent making the same mistakes over and over again." He insists, too, that certain qualities of information make for richer or poorer feedback loops. It does no good, he says, "if the communication becomes too frequent, too verbose, or too esoteric." The message, he adds, is "Pay attention to the people who work in your organization, what they are saying and asking of you. They will let you know whether what you are doing is working for them or not."

Ultimately, the Feedback Challenge requires what organizational theorists call *knowledge management* (Davenport & Prusak, 1998; Rumizen, 2002). The simplest way to explain knowledge management is to say that it involves the assiduous pursuit of an elusive but nonetheless achievable goal. Carla O'Dell and C. Jackson Grayson capture the goal well in the title of their 1998 book: *If Only We Knew What We Know*. That is, if only we knew how to capture both the explicit and tacit knowledge of the smallest units of the organization, for example, a teacher's practice, or of the organization's most remote units, for example, a school operating far from design headquarters, and then scale up that knowledge for wider use.

## DISTANT MIRROR: EATING WELL IN NEW YORK (AND OTHER PLACES)

*In what follows, we view all the strategies (and, implicitly, challenges) we have explored in this and the previous chapter in a distant mirror. Instead of school designing, we focus mostly on food retailing. The purpose of a distant mirror is to aid reflective transfer by stripping a case of nearly all its context, leaving behind only those basic elements that might be transferable to other contexts. This is one of two distant mirrors in the book. The second concludes Chapter 4.*

In the 1st year of our study of BP's going to scale, there was a replication failure in New York City having to do with a famous grocery store. Suddenly, the lights went out on Sixth Avenue, between 9th and 10th Streets, and the grates came down permanently on the Balducci's there. This was the store where James Beard shopped, the one that defined for many in New York and elsewhere what it means to be a gourmet grocery (*articulation/differentiation*). However, its image had frayed over the previous several years. One of us, visiting the store for some salmon sausage and frissee only 2 nights before the quick closing, thought the place looked terrible (*imagery*).

It was not just that the store was no longer a family operation (the family had quarreled and sold it to a chain called Sutton Place Gourmet) or even that the chain had begun to skimp on varieties of fresh pasta and imported olive oil in order to stock freshly made sandwiches for takeout. It was also that the competition had grown remarkably: Gourmet Garage, the Garden of Eden, Fairway, Grand Central Market, the Union Square farmer's market, Whole Foods, Trader Joe's. Balducci's was no longer the only place to get Serrano ham, Parmigiano Reggiano, or even fresh truffles and pheasant. But an even bigger problem was that the people who worked there no longer seemed to "get it," no longer had the attitude that helped to make the art of shopping for good food accessible (*transparency*), that made shoppers through mere contact with the store and its culture emerge from the shopping experience more confident in their own cooking (*enculturation*). That's what used to happen in Balducci's, but this difference had somehow evaporated amid the effort to replicate the store.

With this original Balducci's gone, some of us had to get good olive oil, for example, fifteen blocks north at the Chelsea Whole Foods. This was the first Whole Foods in New York City (now there are six, with several more in the suburbs). *Cook's Magazine* rates Whole Foods extra virgin olive oil as being as good as olive oil gets, which is a great exaggeration, but nonetheless an image that inspires confidence (*imagery*). Whole Foods is a supermarket chain notably different from others in certain respects, including its organizational design. Fishman (1996) describes its internal Web site (*transparency*) as follows:

> It collects and distributes information to an extent that would be unimaginable almost anywhere else. Sensitive figures on store sales, team sales, profit

margins, even salaries, are available to every person in every location. In fact, the company shares so much information so widely that the SEC has designated all 6,500 employees "insiders" for stock-trading purposes (p. 10).

Whole Foods now has more than 270 stores throughout the United States, Canada, and the United Kingdom, with 54,000 employees. It is the largest retailer of natural and organic foods in the world (www.wholefoodsmarket.com). When this different kind of chain first came to New York, we observed the Whole Foods culture grow here, slowly at first, then pervasively. So, at first, in the way of most supermarkets, members of the checkout "team" still chatted with one another rather than with their customers, as if the customers were no more than the items in their baskets. But that seldom happens anymore at Whole Foods New York (*training* and *coaching*). And meat team members, cheese team members, and grocery team members now go out of their way to assist shoppers in a way that is absolutely unimaginable at Morton Williams or Gristedes—two other supermarket chains in New York.

How did the Whole Foods culture grow in the hostile environs of New York City? The same way that sourdough bread gets made, namely, by means of a starter culture. When a new Whole Foods store is scheduled to open in, say, Santa Fe or Santa Barbara, employees in New York and Seattle are invited to move to the new place for a few months or permanently (*building and networking communities of practice*). They teach the new staff the culture of the organization, even as they learn about and communicate the challenge of adapting the culture to the new context (*coaching*).

Still, scale imposes limits on culture, in the way that Elliot Washor suspected as he mused on the prospect of 44 BP schools, and as Dennis Littky worried when he realized that he would never get to know any of the new BP schools as well as he had got to know the prototype schools in Providence. One of us first got to know Whole Foods in Providence too, in one of its smallest stores on Waterman Street. This is Whole Foods on the scale of the original Balducci's, the one that closed on Sixth Avenue. Walking from produce to fish to bakery is a matter there of mere steps. There are few cashiers, but rarely lines. Not so in New York, where the Chelsea Whole Foods has one long line nearly always, though it moves very fast and feeds into a stunningly plentiful array of tiny cashier counters. Still it is difficult to believe that these Chelsea cashiers like their job as much as the Providence cashiers seem to. And it's much worse at the Union Square Whole Foods, at the heart of New York's food center, and very near several New York University dorms. This is nearly always packed with people. Meanwhile, the Whole Foods in Columbus Circle has a line so long (though also very fast) that it frightens people when they first see it. Then there's the Whole Foods on the Bowery—yes, the Bowery. The store that is some-times called "Whole Paycheck" has one of its biggest stores on a street long known for its association with the destitute, though a street now increas-ingly peopled by the affluent. A chef friend of ours who loves Whole Foods tried this store once and said she would not go back. It's too big to be fun, she said. After a certain point, scale can take a toll on imagery.

Luckily, however, there are still other ways to get good food in New York—including good olive oil. In the second year of our BP study, one of us living in New York received a gift of olive oil. Hand dated, and without a word of English on the label, the bottle seemed straight from Azienda Agricola I Lecci, in the province of Brescia in northernmost Italy. But the shipping package suggested instead that it had come, oddly, from a deli-catessen in Ann Arbor, Michigan: Zingerman's Deli. A few weeks later, Dennis Littky happened to reach into the back pocket of the airline seat in front of him to discover an article about this deli in *Inc. Magazine* (Burlingham, 2003). The title caught his eye: "The Coolest Small Company in America." (See also Burlingham's 2005 book, *Small Giants*.)

Zingerman's Delicatessen was founded in 1982 by Ari Weinzweig and Paul Saginaw. Over the next 10 years or so, they developed it into a suc-cessful company employing more than 100 people, with sales approach-ing $7 million annually, and with a considerable reputation within and beyond Ann Arbor for high-quality sandwiches, brownies, latkes, and so on. As Leslie Brokaw (2003) suggests in another article about Zingerman's, many people in the position of Weinzweig and Saginaw would have begun then to think about franchising the operation. But several factors held them back. One was that they liked being local and unique and felt that some significant part of their success depended on staying both. "It's para-doxical," Weinzweig explained to Brokaw. "You've created something unique—that's why people want to replicate it, but if you actually repli-cated it, it would lose its uniqueness" (p. 36). What Weinzweig and Saginaw decided to do instead was to create a collection of unique companies, linked by the principles animating the delicatessen. At the time Brokaw wrote, the new Zingerman's, made up of linked companies, was 8 years and seven businesses into a 15-year strategic plan, one that calls for the creation of as many as 15 businesses:

> There's the deli, the bakehouse, the mail order unit, a catering operation, and a web site. There's also ZingTrain, a training business that runs seminars in everything from specialty foods and merchandising to staff management. The newest business is a creamery to produce fresh dairy products and get in-volved nationally with groups using traditional methods of making cheese. The next project in development is Zingerman's Roadhouse, an American regional restaurant. (p. 59)

And there is also the nonprofit business, Food Gatherers, which collects leftovers from Ann Arbor–area restaurants and distributes them to food kitchens.

Back in Providence, following the plane trip on which Dennis Littky discovered Zingerman's, he asked the BP staff to consider a redefinition of what *big picture* means. Perhaps it might mean something more than an organization that creates and supports its own schools—many of them, too many of them to know well. Perhaps it could mean an organization that learns continually from its own small set of schools and then in varied other enterprises uses what it learns to press for a radical revisioning of American youth education. Thus on a cold January day, the BP staff warmed to the task of brainstorming categories of "other enterprises" that might link to the BP school, and that might collaboratively advance the ideas animating them, that might make BP more like Zingerman's than Whole Foods. They imagined a publishing house; a curriculum design laboratory in collaboration with other organizations; a design studio focused on, among other things, architecture and furniture for small schools; a new school facilities consulting firm; a speakers bureau, including kids; a facilitator of a network of school design organizations; and a college.

Elliot Washor hadn't been able to attend this meeting, and did not so readily warm to the idea of thinking about the "big picture" in Zingerman terms. That would put too much emphasis, he later told us, on the components of BP schooling rather than on the wholeness of it. "We're *whole-school reform*," he said, and added that the influence of BP ideas depends ultimately on a sufficient number of whole schools. But what is *sufficient*? How much does it depend on concentration, for example, the kind of concentration that BP achieved early on in Providence, versus spread, the kind of spread that Gates funding encouraged? Early in its efforts to move beyond Providence, BP talked about establishing a BP school in or near every American city with a population of at least 100,000 people. According to the 2000 Census, there are 239 such cities, from Athens, Georgia, to New York City. That is hardly an unachievable goal for a school designer. Still, by 2003, 239 seemed too many schools, to both Littky and Washor.

It would take the partners some time, however, to evolve a different idea of scale—neither Whole Foods nor Zingerman's. The men have a long history of occasionally pulling in opposite directions, working out such tension by talking with each other at length. In this case, they brought the advantage of their new roles to the task; Washor had become the road man by then, living in San Diego, while Littky remained in Providence. Together they had fresh and constant access to the value of both breadth and intimacy. Washor reflected for us much later on the Zingerman dispute. "Dennis was thinking then about how to protect the design," he told us, "while I was saying, 'There are *millions* of kids out there.'" But "what you have to understand," he added, "is that we could easily have switched positions and sometimes did." In the end, they decided that the influence they both sought was not dependent on scale in the ordinary sense, and indeed that too big a scale could make BP schooling merely commonplace rather than influential.

Another imperfect analogy better captures how they ended up: neither Whole Foods nor Zingerman's. Both Whole Foods, despite its name, and Zingerman's, despite its deli, are more food purveyors than food artists. But the kind of influence that Littky and Washor aspired to was aesthetic. Washor's complaint that the Zingerman's path to influence isn't "whole" and Littky's insistence on the ineffable value of "being there" both hint at this quality. And when it comes to food, one looks for aesthetics among restaurants, not markets.

So in another analogy, BP's scaling-up strategy falls somewhere between Danny Meyer's restaurants and Wolfgang Puck's. Danny Meyer is one of the great champions of eating local. Bo Burlingham chronicles Meyer's Union Square Hospitality Group in *Small Giants*, the 2005 book that also portrays Zingerman's. Union Square is the place—above, we called it New York's food capital—where the second New York Whole Foods market opened. More than anyone else, Meyer made it the "food capital" by opening Union Square Café in 1985, by promoting what was then the square's small farmer's market as a major source of its chef's ingredients, and then by opening other restaurants nearby. The café opened to an acclaim that remains strong many *Zagats* later (*Zagat* is the annual restaurant guide that keeps tabs on quality and popularity). A decade later, Meyer opened Gramercy Tavern in the same neighborhood, then Eleven Madison Park, Tabla, and Blue Smoke—all quite different from each other, all superb and popular, all with chefs who shop for locally grown or raised food in the Union Square market. At the same time, Meyer turned down many offers to open restaurants elsewhere, for example, in Los Angeles or Las Vegas. He wanted to be able to walk to work and visit all his restaurants within the same evening. By 2008, he had eleven of them, counting Shake Shack in Madison Square Park, and the Modern at the Museum of Modern Art some 40 blocks north (Meyer, 2006). Meanwhile, on the other side of this *other* analogy, Wolfgang Puck is the Austrian-turned-Californian celebrity chef whose fusion instincts made him an originator of new American cuisine. He earned the distinction before scaling up, on the basis of a single restaurant in Los Angeles named Spago. Today there are Spagos in Vail; Maui; and most famously, Las Vegas. Indeed, Puck transformed Vegas dining with five other restaurants. Plus he has six cookbooks; a Wolfgang Puck product line that runs from canned soups and frozen pizza to cookware and cooking spray; and 26 Wolfgang Puck airport cafés, from

Newark to Seattle. Who would settle for a between-flight Big Mac and Coke when you could have a salmon-and-caviar thin-crust pizza and a glass of California chardonnay?

The Danny Meyer side of this analogy accentuates both "wholeness" *and* "being there," and exploits "localness" in the way that Littky set out to do in Providence. The Wolfgang Puck side accentuates adventure—the way Washor did by moving to San Diego—and also diversity of enterprise, though its scale is far short of Starbucks. Thus at BP, Littky and Washor slowed down the pace of BP growth by renegotiating their contract with the Gates Foundation. Elliot Washor now calls their scaling-up "small-scale scale."

Today, the partners think that BP will end up with far more than the 44 schools that Washor once worried about, and fewer than the 239 they once considered desirable. However, they have not definitively ruled out getting much bigger as the result of the relatively informal relationships they have cultivated (as contrasted with formal franchising and contracting) with, for example, independent school designers in Israel, the Netherlands, and Australia. And BP has made a start on its Zingerman (correction: Wolfgang Puck collection of other enterprises). It runs conferences on topics that attract a variety of educators and others, for example, on the role of hands in learning. It also has a network of school designers, called the Alternative High School Initiative. Funded by the Gates Foundation, this network of youth development organizations have designed nontraditional schools. Its mission is "to inspire and assist communities in providing all students— regardless of their race, socio-economic status or learning styles—with a rigorous educational experience culminating in the opportunity to receive a school diploma and attend college" (Alternative High School Initiative, n.d.). The network includes, among others, YouthBuild USA, Good Shepherd Services, Diploma Plus, and the Black Alliance for Educational Options.

BP is also currently negotiating with several potential partners concerning the creation of Big Picture College. In Chapter 6, we explore BP's determination to wrestle with what we call the Mindset Challenge or common-sense idea of high schooling. There we mention also that the common-sense sharp distinction between high school and higher education is relatively recent, and we suggest that it may possibly be pernicious in its impact on youth and the economy. In late 2008, Elliot Washor told us that "it doesn't matter what you call our schools—career and technical academies in Rhode Island, continuation schools or early college in California, even a residential job corps school or a carpentry school. What matters are the distinguishers, and the principle of going life to text instead of the other way around." That's at least a little like what Danny Meyer might have said about his decision to open a shake shack, or Wolfgang Puck about his decision to get into the airport restaurant business.

# 4

# The Resource Challenge: Six Dimensions and a Distant Mirror

Yes, there are seven challenges, and they all matter. But in the end it comes down to managing numbers 6 and 7: the Resource Challenge and the Political Challenge. Fail here and you fail, period. This is one reason we give each of these challenges its own chapter. The other reason is that they are both so complicated.

The Resource Challenge is *the* most complicated of the challenges to understand because it has six different dimensions. Here is our list of them, phrased as assertions:

### DIMENSIONS OF THE RESOURCE CHALLENGE

1. There are *three* resources and they make a combustible mix.
2. Resource needs interact.
3. Resources must be obtained *and* managed.
4. School designers have to manage resources within an environment lacking good indicators of effectiveness.
5. The demands of the resource challenge vary with the phases of replication.
6. Meeting these demands puts strains on organizational culture, leadership, and theory of action.

In the first half of the chapter, we illustrate each of these dimensions of the Resource Challenge, and offer advice for how to deal with them. Then, in the concluding half, we look at the challenge in a more holistic way—from the perspective of a distant mirror. It consists of a narrative about starting out, scaling up, and losing control. Instead of being about school design, it's about ice cream.

## DIMENSION 1:
## THREE RESOURCES MAKE A COMBUSTIBLE MIX

The first dimension of the Resource Challenge concerns the fact that three different kinds of resources are involved. Successful start-ups and scale-ups in schooling by design require a mix of *new money, ambitious talent,* and *cutting-edge ideas.* This is a combustible mix. We mean this in a good way. That is, the mix is capable of generating substantial energy given the right spark. That energy can be used for startup and for scale-up. The spark involves what Jerry Kitzi (2001) calls "opportunity recognition." The opportunity might take the form of an interested "investor"—maybe the kind of person Malcolm Gladwell (2000) calls a connector. Or it might be a call for proposals, one that stimulates the formation of a creative team. Or it might even involve the formation of a movement, one capable of coalescing ideas, people, and money. The following brief histories of the two school designers we highlight in this book illustrate this process.

*The Big Picture Company* came into existence because voters in Providence approved a bond issue to build a new vocational and technical high school (new money); because Dennis Littky and Elliot Washor were looking for a new challenge (ambitious talent); because Ted Sizer brought them both to the new Annenberg Institute for School Reform at Brown University, inviting them to think big about what they wanted to do together next (cutting-edge ideas); and because Stanley Goldstein, the founding CEO of the CVS drugstores and an important figure in the Rhode Island business community, as well as Charlie Mojkowski, a key consultant for the State Department of Education, sensed an opportunity for Rhode Island education (start-up spark). They helped broker Littky's and Washor's entrée to the state's educational and political establishment. Their championship of the idea of using the bond money to build several small and innovative vocational schools rather than one big conventional one was critical to forming the coalition of statewide and grassroots leaders that got the Met going. Later there was the invitation from the Bill and Melinda Gates Foundation to replicate the Met in other places (scale-up spark), and multiple grants from Gates as well as other funders (more new money).

*Expeditionary Learning Schools* (*ELS*) is the inheritor of a century of ideas about experiential education that stretch back to the European educator Kurt Hahn, founder of Outward Bound (cutting-edge ideas then and now). ELS itself emerged from Outward Bound's Education/Urban Initiative, supported by a grant from the DeWitt Wallace–Reader's Digest Foundation in 1990. The initiative aimed to develop analogues for the educational power of a wilderness program, and to bring them into urban schools. Key shapers in this period (ambitious talent) included Meg Campbell of the Harvard–Outward Bound Project, a key site of the Education/Urban Initiative; former Harvard education dean Paul Ylisaker; the educational historian Thomas James; Jerry Pieh, son of the founder of Minnesota Outward Bound and a long-experienced school leader; Diana Lam, former superintendent of the Chelsea, Massachusetts, schools; and, of course, Greg Farrell. The latter brought not only his unique experience as the founder of the first Outward Bound–inspired urban school, in Trenton, New Jersey, in 1965, but also the ties he had formed to the philanthropic community over twenty years as executive director of the Fund for the City of New York.

In 1992, Outward Bound responded to a request for proposals issued by the New American Schools Development Corporation, later renamed New American Schools (NAS), for teams interested in developing, testing, and going to scale with "break the mold school designs." Farrell remembers that Outward Bound was at first dubious about its capacity to deliver all that NAS was seeking in the teams it proposed to fund. But "Outward Bound casts you back on your own resources and you find that you have some." And it was "just bait to an Outward Bound person," he added, "to say that you have more to offer than you think" (start-up spark). Indeed, Outward Bound's Expeditionary Learning proposal was one of eleven winning proposals from among approximately 800 submitted (new money).

During 1993–1994, ELS began with ten demonstration projects undertaken in collaboration with schools in New York City; Boston; Denver; Portland, Maine; and Dubuque, Iowa, bringing on still more ambitious talent rooted in these places. Two of the ten schools were created to be ELS schools, while the other eight used the ELS ideas and supports as elements of a transformation effort. The NAS community of other school designers, researchers, and consultants added still more intellectual resources, including novel conceptions of financial resources and how to gain them (more cutting-edge ideas). In 1997, Congress passed the Obey-Porter legislation, which stoked the demand side of the emerging market for new school designs by committing up to $50,000 a year for three years to support a school's adoption of a "comprehensive reform model" (new money). Then in 2003, the Gates Foundation awarded ELS a $12.6 million grant to focus on new small high school development (scale-up spark). An additional grant from Gates in 2007, plus grants from the Kaufmann Foundation and Stuart Foundation (more new money) led to an ELS network of affiliated schools in 29 states involving 4,300 teachers serving 45,000 students (Expeditionary Learning Schools, 2007).

## DIMENSION 2:
## RESOURCE NEEDS INTERACT

Getting enough money may depend a lot on having the right people in place with hands-on design skills and fund-raising expertise. But getting these people may depend on having enough money to pay them. Meanwhile, getting good ideas in place that are adequate to the work, and articulating these ideas in ways that remote users can understand, depend on having people with yet other skill sets and also on having the money to support the expensive work they do.

Managing the risks and trade-offs here were a constant part of the management environment at Big Picture during our study. For a long time, the organization stayed small and local and depended on a staff of smart, young generalists. Then it rapidly increased the number of schools it worked with—because it wanted to be influential, and had been invited by the Gates Foundation to be influential. This expanded its financial base, because the Gates funding formula was tied to the number of schools. With the new money, BP was able to recruit high-quality specialized staff and to work hard on the cultivation and dissemination of ideas. In the process, it acquired some slack in all three resource categories, enough to cover inevitable pockets of deficit. So it relied on dollars from unfilled positions or other budget savings to cover core costs, and it got by for awhile with a bookkeeper until it found the right CFO and with intuition about what makes a BP school BP until it gained enough experience to spell this out. This is a kind of "rash" maneuvering that all growing companies, whether nonprofit or for profit, have to learn to do well.

Schools starting up have to learn to do it well also. But at this level, interaction effects can be more dangerous, threatening a kind of "poor get poorer" slide that can require rescue or lead to failure. School designers are thus always in the rescue business too. For example, one of the new BP schools starting up in a big city had a very hard time getting the financial machinery of its district even to recognize that it existed. "Aren't you a charter school?" someone downtown asked. The school is not. The consequence of this neglect was that several months into its first school year, the school had no computers in its computer lab, no copier, and a fax machine that "dialed" local calls only. There was a laptop at the school that someone brought from home and students used for word processing, but there was no Internet connection and thus no chance that the students, or their advisors (at least at work), could access the ideas and materials available to them at Big Picture Online. Then when the principal finally got a resource connection established with downtown, he was suddenly asked to spend $150,000 in 3 days, with purchases restricted to school supplies and instructional materials. Naturally, he made mistakes. "Do you need any paper clips?" he asked us on a visit, implying he had plenty to go around.

Meanwhile, this new principal of a new school based on an unusual design, one that nobody else in his district had ever experienced, was also new to the job of being principal. So he had to learn general school management skills on the job (as new principals always do), even as he continued to learn about the BP school design and the intricacies of a very intricate district. Looking for teachers to hire as the new school's first advisors, he told us that he had especially searched for people who could believe in the ideas of the school and in the potential of the poor and underskilled kids the school attracted, who could connect well with these kids one-on-one, who seemed to have good problem-solving skills, and who were bilingual. Although he hired well according to these criteria, he ended up with a staff of two 1st-year teachers (*advisors*, in BP parlance). Not only did they have to learn on the job how the BP school design works, they also had to learn basic group management techniques. Of course, if there had been experienced BP advisors already at the school, or perhaps even nearby, or if the principal himself had been a BP advisor, or had had enough money to hire a third teacher who was experienced, then the resource gap would not have been so disadvantageous.

Interrelated resource shortages put great demands not only on principals and others at start-up sites like this one, but also on the designer's backup support systems. In this case, BP supplied emergency coaching (from a Met advisor flown in to help), ongoing support for the principal from other BP staff in person and by phone and e-mail, and some political intervention with the district.

Meanwhile, the principal told us in this difficult 1st year that he held fast to two strategic ideas he learned in his BP training. The first is that even a toehold on one resource can help over time to bring in others. So the principal hired good support staff: a security guard, an office manager/secretary, and a maintenance worker, all from the community. They liked kids, and they talked with them, not just about the kids' lives but also about their LTIs. The principal told us he hoped they would help the school be noticed and appreciated in the community and that this would in turn bring in a steady stream of students and LTI mentors, as well as needed political cover. The second strategic idea that got him through the year, and that he said Littky and Washor impressed on him again and again, is that everything depends on making connections. In the hopes of helping to fill his resource gaps, the principal sought out a neighborhood priest who works with gang-related youth; in turn, the priest connected him to other important neighborhood resource providers, including a college professor who helped the school develop a video production program. In an interview with us, Elliot Washor called this "going from connection to connection to connection," and he claimed that it is the best way to solve the Resource Challenge in all its dimensions.

It's important to note in this regard that resource-minded connecting is built into the BP design. That is, being a BP school requires having a group of "investors" who have agreed to participate personally as a voluntary internship mentor or to open their workplace as an internship site or both. These people not only have become acquainted with the BP design and the ideas about teaching and learning that undergird it, but also have implicitly "bought into it" with their time and energy. Their names become powerful lures to other investors, including financial ones.

Reflecting on the Resource Challenge, our dialogue partner Howard Wollner tells us that the challenge is "common to most businesses, and certainly was always a challenge for Starbucks." For example, he says that Starbucks also needed to figure out a "success profile" for its hires in order to avoid "having to regroup too often due to hiring errors." He tells us that "as the company grew, it hired managers from more traditional multiunit operators, for example, McDonald's, Burger King, and Taco Bell. These new hires were well seasoned in the operation of small footprint, multiunit stores, but to fit in and succeed at Starbucks, they had to be open to trying new methods of operating, and they had to be willing to embrace the unique culture." Whenever new hires, even the most skilled, "resisted the culture or relied solely on their proven experience elsewhere, they invariably washed out."

## DIMENSION 3:
## RESOURCES MUST BE OBTAINED *AND* MANAGED

Greg Dees (2001) writes that entrepreneurs by definition "find ways to do more with less, and persuade others to provide resources on favorable terms" (p. 63). This is why, despite chronic scarcity of resources, we call entrepreneurs resource*ful*. It is important to note, however, that such resourcefulness involves adapting to a very different funding environment today from the one that existed merely a decade ago. It's one that insists that *obtaining* is not enough, that managing matters just as much. And it insists also that people and ideas are central to both. Three resources, two tasks. This is why this dimension of the Resource Challenge is so complicated.

Marc Dean Millot (2004) traces the roots of today's funding environment to disappointing results among the first investments in the cycle of school reform that followed the release of *A Nation at Risk* (National Commission on Excellence in Education, 1983). First investor foundations often saw the innovations they funded fade with the last of the funding. Of course, many things may account for this fading, including especially the Political Challenge that we explore in the next chapter. But the funding community focused on the challenge that seemed most within its sphere of influence and most amenable to rational solutions. So while some of these disappointed first investors got out of the business of school reform completely, others started to shift emphasis from merely making grants to managing them.

The new emphasis on management of resources for innovation led also to the rise of nonprofit investment organizations like the one that Millot himself founded in 1999 under the auspices of New American Schools. It was called the Education Entrepreneurs Fund and changed NAS from an intermediary grant maker into a loan maker. A good example today of this new breed of funder is the New Schools Venture Fund. It invites both foundations and individual philanthropists to invest in its "portfolio" of education projects, which it then supports with venture capital and management consulting. Instead of calling for grant proposals, it solicits business plans from prospective clients. New Schools Venture Fund has already invested nearly $80 million in its project portfolio and is currently raising an additional $125 million (Flanigan, 2006). The projects include educational support organizations like Teach for America, which recruits recent college graduates to teach in hard-to-staff urban and rural schools, and Revolution Foods, a for-profit company that partners with Whole Foods and other organizations to serve healthy food to kids in the San Francisco Bay–area schools. Projects also include many of the nation's most important charter school management organizations, like Achievement First, High Tech High, Green Dot Public Schools, and KIPP. Both these investment emphases suggest that the shift in the funding environment reflects a deeper shift toward a market-based conception of schooling, one that aims through contracts and charters to generate previously unimaginable supply and demand opportunities.

In addition to foundations and venture capital firms that help school designers and other education projects both obtain and manage resources, there are other firms that focus only on the managing. For example, in the 2nd year of our study, BP got help in managing its resources from the Bridgespan Group, a nonprofit consulting firm that works with other nonprofits. Generally such organizations concern themselves with human resource management as well as financial resource management, but some deal as well with knowledge resource management, or what is often called simply *knowledge management* (Rumizen, 2002).

Such resource consulting groups tend to promote the rational models characteristic of strategic planning in noneducation and for-profit sectors. Typical of these is the model that Greg Dees and his coauthors (Dees, Emerson, & Economy, 2001) recommend for achieving what they call a resource-smart management system: Focus first on "desired results," then plan backward to imagine necessary capabilities, operating structure, economic model, and finally resource needs (p. 65). Such good management advice can help, but we think that school designers shouldn't expect that it will eliminate messiness and uncertainty. Strategic planning can never fully predict where meaning and doing will end up or obviate the periodically painful process of realigning them.

The reason is the complication of three resources and two tasks all operating in real time. The result is that school designers scaling up inevitably find themselves out of "task balance." They may obtain too much of a resource too soon, or too much of what is less needed (for example, paper clips), or just what *is* needed but without the distribution systems in place to get it to *where* it is needed. When they hit on a big grant or meet a deep-pocket philanthropist or political leader eager to create better schools in Detroit or the South Bronx, they ignite great energy that is also hard to handle at first. It may require the rapid creation of new accounting systems and management information systems capable of integrating operational and financial management. Moreover, the designers can also expect from time to time to get out of task balance with regard to human resources and knowledge resources. So they may successfully recruit, hire, train, and coach all the people they need, but flounder in matching skills and talents to problems and tasks and struggle to build good infrastructures for support and supervision. Similarly, they may work hard and successfully to meet the knowledge resource aspects of the Resource Challenge by tuning into outside ideas, capturing inside insights, and using both to generate fresh perspectives; but they may struggle to invent systems able to put the ideas to use at the right places and in time to do the most good. That is, the power of their ideas may overwhelm the capacity of their Web sites and intranets, their print and video materials, and their coaching systems. Or the imbalance at times may go the other way: fancy systems but still weakly articulated ideas.

Reflecting on these first dimensions of the Resource Challenge, our dialogue partner Greg Farrell recalls the rich mix of intellectual resources that ELS gained from its incubation at New American Schools among the other funded school designers:

> One of the great things about NAS was being convened with all these other cats doing school reform in different ways. Bob Slavin, of Roots and Wings [and Success for All], was hilariously funny,

good, and generous with his experience. And there was Sally Kilgore of Modern Red Schoolhouse, Linda Gerstle of ATLAS Communities, the guys at CONNECT. We learned a lot from each other, and there was a lot of exchange, like "How much does it cost you to put a person in a school for a day? How much do you pay consultants? What's the ratio of your what to your whatever?" NAS could have made more of this exchange power, but they made enough of it so that I was always happy to go to the meetings. And Tom Glennan and Sue Bodily [of Rand, which conducted the ongoing evaluation of NAS] gently held our feet to the fire of our promises, and we learned a lot from that.

Farrell also recalls the culture shock involved in coming to think about financial resources from a business perspective:

There was the point when we were suddenly all going on the market, and we had the Rand guys there, and they were trying to plot our costs. Bruce Goldberg's costs—from CONNECT—were off the charts, but he just laughed and told them that he was operating in Swiss francs. And Slavin said that when it comes to economics, his guy was Marx—Groucho not Karl. When Groucho was asked how much something cost, he'd say, "How much do you have with you right now?" You see we were used to the old philanthropy, but this was a time when the new philanthropies were coming on, and NAS helped us prepare for them. They helped us gain business sense, become program managers, make strategic plans.

They also helped Farrell and the other NAS school designers take account of the next dimension of the Resource Challenge.

## DIMENSION 4:
## GOOD INDICATORS OF EFFECTIVENESS ARE LACKING

The fourth dimension of the Resource Challenge concerns the inadequacy of school-level indicators to guide the smart allocation of resources. Together with the last dimension, this one delivers a one-two punch. It means that school designers have to spend an inordinate amount of time and effort inventing what entrepreneurs in other sectors can take for granted.

New school designers need to get the right resources to the right places at the right time to support the development of their schools. When their overall operations are small and their staffs generalist and highly integrated, they can visit their pilot schools and make more or less collective judgments about what the schools need. As their operations scale up, however, the designers lose the opportunity for frequent eyes-on monitoring and also lose the capacity to pool judgment calls. This is when indicator systems become very important. By paying close attention to sensitive indicators of their new schools' effectiveness—ones highly correlated with essential design features—and by standardizing resource allocations to what the indicators tell them, school designers can operate smartly at scale.

The problem is that readily available indicators of school effectiveness are typically crude. For students' intellectual engagement, there are average daily attendance reports; for their intellectual achievement gains, there are standardized test results that are generally not longitudinal; for their moral development or citizenship or sense of safety, there is the number of yearly police incidents or some similar measure; for school progress in narrowing achievement gaps, there are the No Child Left Behind target reports, which for small schools with necessarily small numbers in population subgroups are really statistical fluctuations rather than indicators; and for the quality of the lives students live outside schools, there are the free and reduced-price lunch statistics.

Some school districts and school designers are working hard to change this. However, Edison Schools founder Chris Whittle's observation remains true—that Federal Express and UPS know much more about the packages they ship than American schools know about their students (Chubb, 2004). If the schools need richer indicators—and they do—school designers (or those who contract with them) have to invent or adapt other measures: student work samples, parent and student satisfaction surveys, school visitation protocols, longitudinal value-added analyses, home and community surveys, follow-up studies of graduates, and so on. School designers have to build such indicators into the school design itself and into the systems that network the schools and teach the design. This means that the school must be designed for research capacity—must be designed to be collectively mindful of its own effectiveness, and to take action as needed to redirect its efforts. It also means that the entire school design enterprise must function to tune its school-based communities of practice to best practice (as this is defined by design) and to audit the results on a continual basis. Developing such built-in measures and external auditing systems demands and consumes resources, both human and financial, that are in short supply. On the other hand, *not* developing such measures eats up resources too. Without better indicators, schools have no easy means of self-regulating, and thus the designer has to engage in the most costly form of management, namely, direct supervision (Chubb, 2004).

Our dialogue partner Howard Wollner suggests, however, that indicators are both crucial and overrated. "Starbucks found," he says, that "what got measured got done." But, he added, "this held true only until the number of metrics became too voluminous, and then it became very random as to what was important." He advocates identifying "key measures, few in number, that can accurately indicate progress or alignment with the mission and purpose of the organization." He acknowledges, however, that it can be difficult at first to think in such terms. "Early strategic plans at Starbucks were rudimentary in their formulation," he says. "Still, these plans did provide a road map and allowed the organization to measure itself against certain benchmarks." And eventually, Starbucks invested in third-party strategic planners. One was Jim Collins, the coauthor of *Built to Last* (Collins & Porras, 1994) and *Good to Great* (Collins & Porras, 2001). "His advice was critical," Wollner says, "in setting the vision, core values, and core purpose for the company. And these led the management team at the time to the conclusion that Starbucks could indeed become a global brand well before there was a proven international business model or plan."

Our other dialogue partner, Greg Farrell, is refreshingly honest about the tortuous route that school designers travel when they try to invent the indicators they need to be accountable:

> We don't have enough confidence yet to go public with the ratings that ELS school designers assign to the schools they work with. On a management team level, we sometimes discuss them and say, "This can't be right. That school seems better than that. I was in that school last week and that doesn't make sense to me." There are lots of issues: interrater reliability, interpretation, easy and tough graders. We have to reconcile these ratings with something that makes sense to keen observers on the ground. But we're getting there. It's better than it was, and I think pretty soon we'll be able to refer to the ratings on the Core Practices Implementation Review with confidence. And meanwhile, our reviews have moved us in the direction of being tighter —more explicit.

## DIMENSION 5: DEMANDS VARY BY PHASE

The fifth dimension of the Resource Challenge involves the fact that different phases of scale demand different approaches to resource management. For example, a school designer probably *should* share financial resources with prototype clients—resources that may come from founda-tion or corporate sources. In the earliest phase of scaling up, these pioneers are really codesigners rather than clients in the ordinary sense. Later, how-ever, such sharing of resources with clients may prove counterproductive. It may shield everyone involved from understanding the true costs of adopting the design, may weaken the school designer's efforts to develop a real-cost accounting system, and may actually devalue the design in the clients' eyes (Tucker, 2004).

The demand for human resources also varies qualitatively across phases of a replication effort. Thus at first, during the hands-on phase of working with prototype sites, the school designer may need generalists who can do everything, from coach new principals effectively to prepare mate-rials and raise funds. Later, such functions as coaching and material prepa-ration and fund-raising are likely to need specialists at various levels. For example, as they scale up, some school designers move from a system of headquarters-based coaches to one using a combination of local school coaches, regional trainers of coaches, and headquarters-based designers of coaching strategy.

Meanwhile, at the school level, too, the different phases of develop-ment may require different kinds and degrees of human resource. For example, the early phases of the first BP start-ups put enormous and enor-mously varied demands on principals. These principals felt pressure to find political and financial angels. Most had to find and renovate space. All had to hire whole staffs and educate staff members (along with students, par-ents, mentors, and others) in the BP ideas, even while still educating them-selves. They also had to negotiate all the politics that attend doing anything different in education, from convincing a superintendent that some report-ing requirement is incompatible with the BP design to figuring out what to do about state testing requirements or (to reassure parents ahead of time) what to do about state university admissions requirements. Then, once their schools opened, the principals had to continue doing all the above, plus create an accountable learning community, a respectful school culture, and an efficient set of operations using the BP materials and structures. All these tasks were more onerous because the BP school is like few others inasmuch as it draws substantially on the learning resources of the larger commu-nity and uses numerous structural and cultural elements unique in Ameri-can schooling.

Today, new BP principals in new BP schools still feel these pressures, and the BP coaches who work with them still report lots of gaps between these new principals' skill sets and the demands of the job. It may indeed be worse now because the dollars that used to be available for a full year of principal preparation have dried up. On the other hand, new BP principals in established schools have far less of a learning curve, and there are now many established schools. Moreover, BP schools today are increasingly clustered, for example, in Rhode Island, California, Michigan, and Colorado. This means that the learning needs of their principals, advisors, parents, and other stakeholders can be more efficiently addressed. It also means that new principals may more likely be drawn from the ranks of experienced advisors in the same or nearby schools.

Even knowledge resources needed for replication vary by phase. In the earliest phases, the most valuable knowledge resources may be those that help illuminate design issues and site-level implementation issues. Later, the most valuable may be those that help illuminate system issues related to communication, training, or resource allocation. Early on, BP especially needed ideas related to the development of materials and training procedures that captured the design in action. Later it needed ideas related to the costing out and the marketing of these materials and training procedures, as well as ideas about coaching and training at a national level.

At the school level also, different knowledge resources are needed at different levels of school development. This is evident in a comparison of what the newest BP schools need versus what the longer-established Met campuses need. The latter still hire new staff, of course, and these newcomers need access to basic ideas and materials, but the continuing staff and leadership need knowledge resources that push practice deeper. While Elliot Washor took on the responsibility of chief itinerant coach for the larger network of BP schools, Dennis Littky hunkered down at the Met, where he continues to orchestrate the effort there to generate and allocate knowledge resources sufficient to pushing practice deeper. The working assumption is that this effort is crucial to establishing the Met as a genuine lab school for the network, and so crucial to the overall replication effort.

Reflecting on this dimension of the Resource Challenge, Howard Wollner again says it's common in business and had to be faced at Starbucks. For example, businesses starting up need people who can handle multiple areas of responsibility. "This allows for growth to continue," he says, "without necessarily having to scale up resources beyond what can be afforded or managed. But once critical scale is reached, it is common to split functions into narrower and deeper responsibilities that can support the next phase of growth." He adds, "Once it was clear that the number of Starbucks stores would easily exceed early projections, hiring people who had run much larger organizations became critical, so that when Starbucks reached the larger store count targets, there were people in place who had been there and done that."

On the other hand, our other dialogue partner, Greg Farrell, warns against expecting the kinds of shifts we noticed at BP to be as sequential as we may have suggested above. His experience at ELS is that resource demands were more "additive." At later points in scaling up, he explains, you still need resources you needed earlier, but now you need others, too, in order to accomplish additional tasks brought on by scale.

## DIMENSION 6:
## MEETING THE CHALLENGE STRAINS CULTURE, LEADERSHIP, AND THEORY OF ACTION

To accommodate shifts in resource demands during scale-up, a school designer must periodically add some organizational functions and adjust others. This may involve deep changes in culture and leadership and may lead to explicit or implicit shifts in the organization's theory of action. The strains are inevitable. The consequences of the strains depend on how they are managed.

Marc Dean Millot says that as the New American Schools affiliates scaled up in the 1990s, they found themselves having to change their organizational culture from that of a think tank to that of a professional services firm (Millot, 2004). This meant adopting the operations and attitudes of a fee-for-service company, hiring specialists to oversee the quality of particular services and their delivery systems, and focusing more on the stability of the school design than on its evolution.

Signs of a similar transformation were evident at BP as we studied it. Evident too were signs of resulting dislocation and resistance. As we said above, BP experienced substantial staffing changes on our watch. At first, it opted for increased specialization within a more hierarchical reporting system (with staff reporting to directors in such areas as school development, communications, research, and financial operations). The new managers, including a managing director, pressed for rational planning, budgeting models, role definition, and standard operating procedures.

The rationale for such changes was that the originally flat BP staffing arrangement, with its reliance on relatively young and inexperienced staff, fluid job descriptions, and invent-as-you-go operations, seemed ill-suited to the design support needs of 60 schools scattered across the United States— an often-cited goal in those days. The task was too big, it was thought, and the financial resources too slim to tolerate such a degree of organizational slack. Yet nearly everyone acknowledged that this slack had been a wellspring of BP creativity.

Of course, BP did not turn over its staff in one sweep. Thus staff members used to an apparently fading organizational culture interacted somewhat uneasily one year with those expected to create a new one. Some of the former reported the loss of an organization that had once felt more democratic in terms of the generation and allocation of resources, one where they had greater voice. And some of the newcomers reported resistance to the new reporting structures and protocols. Then BP began reversing course. At the fall 2003 staff retreat, Dennis Littky complained that "as we get bigger, people get pushed into being solely in charge of something." He prefers, he said, "this thing I keep reading about—synchronicity. It's about dance, but it applies to us too." When at one point in the retreat he called for "reinventing ourselves," it seemed a call for yet another organizational dislocation. Indeed, it was. We wrote in Chapter 3 of how Littky proposed that BP take what we called the Zingerman's path, of how Washor balked, and of how they dealt with the tension. In the process they jettisoned some of the specialists they had hired—including the managing director.

Our dialogue partner Howard Wollner reminds us that all the challenges are recurring ones. Starbucks faced this dimension of the Resource Challenge starting up, he says, and it faces it now. Early in the process of Starbucks growth to its current scale, CEO "Howard Schultz could meet with the whole management team in the offices that were located directly over the first new roasting plant built in the late 1980s. Not only could you smell the coffee there, you could look directly down on the roasting plant floor." But then, much to Schultz's consternation, Wollner continues, "Support center activities had to move away from the roasting plants as Starbucks grew. Of course, we did numerous things to ensure the culture stayed intact, and much of it worked." Still, in February 2007, Wollner adds, "Schultz wrote that memo to his management team, and it admitted dilution of the Starbucks Experience." There had been too many incremental changes in the stores and the products, and "when aggregated over time, they led to less intimacy with customers, a loss of the coffee aroma, stores that felt more generic, and partners who were less engaged with customers." Schultz called for a "return to basics, a focus on training, and less competition for products and programs within the stores."

## DISTANT MIRROR:
## ICE CREAM AND SCHOOL DESIGN

*Periodically throughout our study of Big Picture Learning, cofounder Dennis Littky told us he worried that the process of going to scale could cause BP to lose control of its own ideas. He didn't want to operate by contractual remote control—without opportunity for exercising his "touch" and feeling every school's "push back." "Should we really have 60 schools?" he asked once. "Wouldn't 20 be enough?" When he and his partner, Elliot Washor, told one of their intellectual mentors, Seymour Sarason, that they had been funded by the*

*Gates Foundation to scale up the BP school design, Sarason told them, "Give back the money. Give it right back."*

*In what follows we explore Dennis Littky's concern and the rationale behind Seymour Sarason's advice through an odd and mostly implicit juxtaposition. In the process, we reprise the dimensions of the Resource Challenge. Having pulled them apart above, we put them back together below.*

## It's About Who *and* What

Ice cream and school design are vastly different enterprises, as are for-profit ventures and not-for-profit ones. Yet anyone who knows even a little bit about Ben & Jerry's on the one hand, and BP on the other, will sense an interesting fit. (Our sources of material on Ben & Jerry's are principally Lager [1994], the Ben and Jerry's Ice Cream Web site [www.benjerry.com], Ben & Jerry's own book [Cohen & Greenfield, 1997], and a small number of other sources cited in the text. Because of the obvious limitations of these secondary sources, the reader should not take what we say here as an authoritative analysis of Ben & Jerry's. What we intend is a distant mirror for school designers, constructed of Ben & Jerry's material.)

Both Ben & Jerry's and BP were founded by two oddball guys who met on Long Island and later got connected more or less indissolubly in New England. Their ventures resemble each other too, in ambition and in a somewhat quixotic commitment to values that set them apart from the mainstream. Both ventures are playful in ways intended partly to signify this apartness and also to stimulate new ways of thinking about business or schooling: ice creams with names like Cherry Garcia or Brazilian Rainforest Crunch and schools with core features like Pick Me Ups and follow-your-passion internships; stunts like scooping out the world's largest sundae weighing in at 27,102 pounds, then letting it slowly melt away in St. Alban's, Vermont; and holding the launch of the national network of new schools with a "Big Bang" at the training camp of the New England Patriots. It happens too that Ben Cohen and Jerry Greenfield (hereafter referred to as Ben and Jerry) actually physically resemble BP founders Dennis Littky and Elliot Washor.

In starting up, founders are the crucial resource. The ideas that become actionable emerge from their intuition and passion. Founders also raise and invest the founding money and provide sweat equity. This is why memoirs are a staple of both business and education literature, whether Ben and Jerry's memoir (Cohen & Greenfield, 1997) or Dennis's (Littky, 2004). In both these cases, the biography backgrounds an idea, as the subtitles of the books suggest—*Ben & Jerry's: Lead with Your Values and Make Money Too*, and *The Big Picture: Education Is Everyone's Business.*

Joel Spolsky (2000) says, however, that too much focus on founders can obscure other views of organizational development. He dismisses Fred "Chico" Lager's (1994) account of Ben & Jerry's as business hagiography. Lager is a former CEO of the company. Spolsky claims that whatever the men's character and intuition, their business developed along one of only two routes possible. Theirs was the organic route, involving limited goals at first and slow growth. This is in contrast to the fast-growth route that Spolsky associates with Amazon.com. Along either route, he says, a scale-up runs into the same challenges, and near the end of the route, the company becomes something other than its founders imagined and more than they can control.

Indeed, as Greg Dees points out, founder's control—so crucial to enterprising nonprofit start-ups—can turn to "founder's syndrome" later on. This is when the leader's interpretation of the founding vision deliberately or inadvertently comes to preclude necessary innovation (Dees et al., 2001, p. 186). Of course, the question remains: What is "necessary"? Burlingham (2005) says of for-profits that founders can stop the march toward bigness and stave off loss of control. They do this partly by keeping their companies private. But what is the counterpart for nonprofits? Seymour Sarason had one answer that he shared with Dennis and Elliot: Be careful of the money you ask for and the money you take.

## Starting Up

In 1978, Ben and Jerry pooled their savings and borrowed a little more in order to invest $12,000 in the transformation of a gas station in Burlington, Vermont, into the first Ben & Jerry's. There they experimented with making ice cream using high-quality ingredients. They sought a rich and dense product. They added chunks of chocolate and other ingredients to help sinus-plagued Ben distinguish the flavors. Their ice cream was well received, bringing in $650 a day and causing long lines at the counter. To keep the customers happy while they waited, the partners created a fun atmosphere. They hired a piano player. They made signs advertising "Today's Orgasmic Flavors."

Meanwhile, they tried hard to get their hired scoopers not to talk too much or scoop too much. This was the company's first human resource problem. Talking among scoopers slowed down the line, and overscooping caused havoc with the supply systems, such as they were (Lager, 1994, pp. 27–28). Neither man relished the role of accountant. Although they sold lots of ice cream, they had little sense of their costs and profits. This was their first financial resource problem. Because of it, they stumbled into what became a signature characteristic: cheap advertising. They adopted a hand-lettered, chunky logo because it was less expensive for a graphic designer friend to draw it than to have it typeset. The designer tried to think like a 5-year-old hungry for ice cream. She urged the guys to repaint the store with bright, primary colors and to add roof art—ice cream cones and coffee cups cut from plywood and painted (p. 30). The look proved effective. But Ben and Jerry supplemented the look with events. They threw end-of-summer celebrations with dancers, jugglers, frog-jumping, and ice cream–eating contests. On their first anniversary, they held a Free Cone Day, and kept up the tradition thereafter.

In their memoir, Ben and Jerry joke that they would have become bagel makers but for the fact that the bagel-making equipment cost too much. They were hippies from the East Village of the early 1970s who wanted to have fun, make a simple living, and contribute to a community. Like some other hippies, they moved to Vermont, where they found themselves almost unexpectedly making ice cream that proved popular. Eventually—after a lot of hard work and trial and error on their part—it began to be profitable too. However, that made Ben uncomfortable. Becoming a successful businessperson seemed in conflict with his hippie values, and the partners had a deal: Neither "would have to do what he really, really didn't want to do" (Cohen & Greenfield, 1997, p. 25).

Then in 1982, Ben had an epiphany. This was just after Jerry had announced his intention to move west, and the partners had put their 4-year-old business on the market. Indeed, they already had an offer for the business, but were ambivalent about its terms. Ben especially felt conflicted. As if to convince himself to accept the offer and move on, he told a friend, "It's just a business, like all others, exploits its workers and the community." But the friend would have none of this. "You don't have to run your business that way," he responded. "If there's something you don't like about the business, change it" (Lager, 1994, p. 57). Soon after, Ben became a businessperson, though one with an ambition out of all proportion to owning an ice cream company with 18 employees. He told the employees that he wanted to prove that business itself, or what he and Jerry in their book call "the most powerful force in society," can be a vehicle for social change (p. 44). This is the idea of the socially responsible corporation, one that links financial prosperity to employee and community prosperity, for example, to higher wages, social activism, and beneficial environmental impact. This was 10 years before the emergence of what Anita Roddick (1991) dubbed value-led business, but Ben & Jerry's was already in pursuit. Ice cream was merely the vehicle.

## Scaling Up

In 1979, Ben and Jerry got into the wholesale ice cream business, with Ben lining up accounts with restaurants in Vermont and upstate New York. To keep both their Burlington scoop shop and their emerging wholesale business in good supply, Ben and Jerry purchased an old textile mill and turned it into an ice cream manufacturing plant. By the summer of 1980, Jerry was overseeing the plant; a manager was running the scoop shop; and Ben was on the road selling and delivering, though no longer just to restaurants. That is because he had seized on a transformative idea. He thought Ben & Jerry's should package ice cream in pints and sell it to grocery stores. Initially, Jerry resisted the idea and invoked the partners' deal—nobody had to do anything that he really, really didn't want to do. But he eventually relented. Their designer friend was called in to create the pint packaging, and she argued for a picture of the two men on the package. This time Ben objected, though he too eventually relented. This would forever brand the product in a highly personalized way. Later, Ben and Jerry both became tireless personalizers.

Within a few months, Ben & Jerry's had 200 on-the-road accounts (mostly mom-and-pop stores) and decided to approach local supermarkets too. Within a year, it had expanded its pint-packing operation beyond the old textile mill and was looking for a distributor. This marked a crucial step in replication and a qualitative shift in management. At about the same time, they began to expand the retail side of their business through franchising—another kind of dependent relationship. The first franchised Ben & Jerry's opened in Shelburne, Vermont, in 1981, and the first out-of-state franchise opened in Portland, Maine, in 1983. Opening a Boston market in the same year required depending on independent distributors as well as franchise owners. Then in 1984, the company took its biggest step into dependence by issuing a public stock offering. It went public for the same reason that companies always do, because it needed new sources of revenue in order to support growth. In particular, it needed the capital to build a new manufacturing plant. But it went public in an oddly local way: The initial public offering was for Vermont residents only.

By 1984, Ben & Jerry's had sales of more than $4 million, a 120% increase over the previous year. In 1985, the company's sales exceeded $9 million, an increase of 143% over the previous year. And in 1986, sales climbed to just under $20 million, more than a 100% jump. When a company grows faster than 100% a year, Joel Spolsky (2000) argues, "it is simply impossible for mentors to transmit corporate values to new hires." Where these values are crucial to product quality, the organization either has to slow growth or figure out a way to beat the odds through cultural power.

Ben and Jerry went for cultural power, or what might be better termed *countercultural power*. It depended on the idea of "linked prosperity." This meant, Lager (1994) explains, that "as the company grew and prospered, the benefits would accrue not just to shareholders, but also to employees and the community. Each constituency's interests were intertwined with the others" (p. 126). Thus Ben & Jerry's established a five-to-one salary ratio, whereby no one could be paid more than five times what the lowest-paid staff member was paid. As Ben put it, this did not mean that it could not offer high salaries to top people, but that it then had to raise all bottom salaries correspondingly. To link outside prosperity to inside prosperity, the company also established the Ben & Jerry's Foundation and instituted the practice of donating 7.5% of its pretax income through the foundation to nonprofit organizations that foster social change.

The new manufacturing plant in Waterbury, Vermont, had been built to accommodate growth, but a result of its vastness was that employees were suddenly spread out. Because size added complexity, the employees also worked in a more departmentalized way. "The up side," writes Lager (1994), "was that more work was getting done. The down side was that as people became more task-oriented, they began to lose their connection to the whole of the organization" (p. 143). To compensate, the company began shutting down production 1 day a month to bring everybody together. The meetings enabled management to communicate about the company (flavors, sales, etc.), and offer information on future plans. The meetings served also as forums to discuss issues and ideas raised by staff and to give line-level employees a voice in strategy and operations development. Through celebrations and other special events, the meeting also passed on the antic culture of the company—the one that had started in the Burlington scoop shop in order to entertain people waiting on line, but had then become a combination operating philosophy and marketing strategy—about being down-home, spunky, inventive, resourceful, and fun. Here it also became a means of building esprit and of holding on to valuable employees.

## Losing Control

In the early 1990s Ben & Jerry's growth policy became a source of tension between Chico Lager, who was then CEO, and Ben, who was still closely involved in management issues. Lager says that Ben believed that if the company got too big, "it risked becoming just another bureaucratic corporation, no different from any other." For his part, Lager thought that this fear created a "mythic horizon, beyond which we never looked," one that precluded sensible long-range planning (pp. 152–153). Their debate ended with both men stepping down and also with the adoption of a mission statement that seemed to resolve some of the differences at stake. Beyond dedicating Ben & Jerry's to the making of "finest quality ice cream" in "innovative flavors" using Vermont dairy products, the mission statement acknowledged the "new corporate concept of linked prosperity." The linkage was between increased benefits to stockholders and employees, on the one hand, and running the business in ways that improve quality of life locally, nationally, and internationally.

Ben's departure made for a huge organizational transition in two respects. First, it meant that the company had to become less intuitive in its product development and marketing strategy. Ben had served as the "official taster" on ice cream development and as the creative force behind the company's marketing. "He had great instincts about what would and wouldn't work," Lager (1994) writes, and Ben & Jerry's relied on these instincts nearly exclusively, never doing market research or test marketing of products. "If Ben thought it was a good idea . . . [Ben & Jerry's] would do it" (pp. 149–50). Meanwhile, what Lager calls Ben's "fanatical commitment to producing a high-quality product" (p. 148) had long been the company's principal vehicle of quality control. He "was a taskmaster and a perfectionist who held everyone to incredibly high standards. He rarely passed out praise and was always focused on what was wrong" (p. 150). However, under Ben's control, the standard remained intuitive and aphoristic. It was tied to his vision of a company whose generosity, spirit, and positive attitude caused everybody to pull together for the common good. Although the company launched the much noticed "Yo, I'm your CEO" contest in 1994 to replace Lager—attracting 22,000 entrants who explained in 100 words or less why they should be the new CEO—the replacement CEO was actually located by a search firm.

This CEO lasted 2 years, and accomplished manufacturing efficiencies, according to the company's Web site. He was followed by one who expanded marketing strategies. Over the next several years, the organization developed formal decision-making processes, long-range planning and budgeting systems, an orientation program for new employees, and an assessment system to evaluate franchise operations—none of which it had had before. It also expanded into many international markets and abandoned its five-to-one salary limit, in order, it said, to attract the caliber of professional managers it needed. By 1999, Ben & Jerry's had net sales of nearly $240 million.

That was also the year that the company announced that it had received "indications of interest" from potential buyers and that it was considering the offers. As the *New York Times* put it in its lead on the story: "A poignant cry is rising from many a Vermonter's heart these days, a plaint for local purity in the face of cold cash and the forces of globalization: 'Say it ain't so, Ben and Jerry'" (Goldberg, 1999, p. 18). Governor Howard Dean protested the possible sale, calling Ben & Jerry's Vermont's signature corporation. He was particularly concerned about the economic impact on the state's dairy farms and the possible loss of the state's premier tourist site, the Ben & Jerry's manufacturing plant. Among other protestors was a street theater group demonstrating outside the Burlington shop, suggesting new flavors like "Chubby Bureaucrat, Funky Money, and Two-faced Swirl." A Web site, www.savebenjerry.com, warned that "gigantic multinational companies are trying to take advantage of Ben & Jerry's undervalued stock price" (Goldberg, 1999, p. 18).

Ben and Jerry themselves were mostly silent in the face of the protests, except that Ben issued a statement saying that he hoped to resolve the tension between his fiduciary obligation as a member of the Ben & Jerry's board to return adequate value to shareholders, and the company's commitment to progressive values. But the savebenjerry Web site was right. What was going on behind the scenes *was* prospecting by multinationals for undervalued stock. From a different perspective, this was another instance of an old dilemma in the company's history—a predictable dilemma of going to scale: how much to depend on others when it comes to resources needed for the job, versus how much to go it alone.

Already this dilemma had led the company to the once unthinkable business decision of letting its old archenemy Häagen Dazs be one of its major distributors. Now the dilemma was threatening a takeover by a major multinational. But the fiduciary obligation that Ben spoke of was real and legally binding. As Vermont's Congress member Bernie Sanders put it with indignation, "The directors of a company could actually be sued because they are responsive to their employees, to local farmers in our state, and to the local economy." The Vermont legislature had passed a law known informally as the Ben & Jerry's law, which declared that a company could consider other factors besides profit in considering a buyout offer. However, the law was untrustworthy for being untested in the courts (Goldberg, 1999, p. 18).

Ben tried to organize a plan that would have divided the company fairly equally between himself; a venture capital firm that describes itself as socially responsible; and an Anglo-Dutch firm called Unilever, whose subsidiaries include Good Humor and Breyer's ice cream companies. In the end, this deal was eclipsed by one that Unilever proffered on its own. This beat the other offer by as much as $10 a share—and at a price considerably above the trading price (Hays, 2000). Ben & Jerry's accepted it.

Ben, who made about $39 million on the deal, was reportedly impressed by the fact that one of the Unilever co-chairmen arrived at negotiations with a knapsack on his back and that he talked about Unilever's sustainable agriculture programs. The Unilever offer included an agreement to maintain a separate Ben & Jerry's board, onetime $5 million payments to both the Ben & Jerry's Foundation and Ben & Jerry's employees, a commitment at least in the short term not to reduce jobs or change the way the ice cream is made, continuation at least for the short term of the 7.5% pretax charitable contribution, and the prospect of Ben & Jerry's concept of "linked prosperity" influencing the practices of the global Unilever with its $44 billion annual sales (Hays, 2000).

"While I would have preferred for Ben & Jerry's to remain independent," Ben said at the announcement, "I'm excited about this next chapter." Then he quoted lines from a Grateful Dead song: "Once in a while you get shown the light in the strangest of places" (Hays, 2000). His allusion was to the possibility that Unilever might buy into "linked prosperity." Meanwhile, both the influence *and* survival of Ben & Jerry's inside Unilever depend on the long-term strength and marketability of the branding that Ben and Jerry gave it. Looking back, it seems clear that this was the only real control the founders ever had.

# 5

# The Political Challenge

All the challenges we explore in this book are at least partly political ones. There is no way you can manage the Fidelity Challenge, for example, if you treat it purely as a philosophical, technical, or symbolic issue. It is all these things, of course, but there are also interests at stake too, interests that tug toward either fidelity or adaptation, and conflicts about where to land on the continuum between them. And we could point out something similar in the Teaching, Ownership, Communication, Feedback, and Resource Challenges too. However, we call the seventh challenge the Political Challenge because it is so manifestly concerned with political calculation and negotiation. It concerns the politics of local adoption. The challenge arises in the early stages of designing, as original ideas encounter real kids, parents, teachers, and policies. Still, there is a natural tendency among school designers to lose track of these first politics amid the other early challenges of schooling by design, such as obtaining resources and articulating for the first time the features of the new design. By the time the designers enter a replication stage, they may be inclined to regard first politics as mere start-up noise. However, they soon learn otherwise.

"When I go to the schools, I'm shocked by how good they are," Elliot Washor told us once about his early visits to the first BP schools outside Providence. "If we didn't have the system stuff to deal with," he added, "we'd be fine." By "system stuff," he meant the politics of local adoption. The remark conveyed the understandable longing of a school designer for an apolitical context. It might be translated as, "On top of having to find resources, develop materials, train people, create a coaching model, network schools, and contract with local entities, you mean I have to put up with politics too?" The answer is yes.

Despite their occasional exasperation with this answer, most school designers come to regard local politics as a source of hope, and BP is no exception. Political noise is the sound of their ideas being taken seriously, the signs of a real school being born, the signs of people on the ground in many different contexts putting their ordinary habits and even their

75

values at risk in order to try something new. In the case of school designs, these risk-takers include those responsible for funding and overseeing schools in a particular context, parents who send their kids to the new and different school, and the kids themselves. Because schooling is one of society's most fundamentally political acts, in the sense that it prepares citizens and also passes on values, negotiating successfully among the diverse interests of stakeholders in new school ventures necessarily requires patient and messy political work. And the intensity of the work is greater in proportion to the difference in the design and the correspondingly lower availability of an easy fallback if the new school fails. One BP coach told us, "A Big Picture school done poorly is a huge, massive disservice to kids. Nothing takes place." More about the difference that difference makes in the next chapter.

What follows here are three stories from the ground, stories of real schools being born. Each documents different political tensions that arose from the particularities of local contexts. Although the stories are unique, the tensions are typical of those we found in other local circumstances. They include the following:

## POLITICAL TENSIONS IN LOCAL DESIGN ADOPTION

- The political burdens of being different
- The burden that reform histories impose on newcomers
- The complications that ensue from different interpretations of the design on the part of people operating at different levels of implementation
- The suspicions that insiders tend to have about outsiders' motives
- The difficulties outsiders encounter when they try to understand inside culture
- The problems of reconciling a new school design with state and local policies
- The conflicts likely to arise between designers and intermediaries

The stories zoom in to particular political issues, deliberately ignoring much else happening at the time, including other challenges besides political ones. And speaking of time, these stories are snapshots in past time. They do not portray the schools as they are today. The stories' usefulness is in their portrayal of some of the ordinary tensions of being born and in the ideas they may spark of how to deal with these tensions.

We follow each story with political commentary, informed by our dialogue partners.

## THE POLITICS OF DIFFERENCE

The setting for this first story is a midsize, midcontinent city with an ambitious reform agenda. A key element of the agenda is an externally funded initiative to replace a number of failing high schools with what the superintendent calls "condo schools," or independently functioning small high schools. As he puts it, "Building size should not dictate size of schools, which is an educational question." The initiative, launched in 2003, was crafted to respond to a concerted effort by leaders of the city's Black and Latino communities to gain better educational opportunities for their youth—and in high schools located within their own neighborhoods. Absent the opportunity to apply for Gates funding, the initiative might have taken some other form, but the city's mayor (who appoints the superintendent) especially found political resonance in the condo idea. "Common sense tells you," she said at a press conference announcing the initiative, "that a small high school will foster stronger relationships between students and faculty." Based on this "common sense," she committed the city to moving fast.

This meant dealing fast with a set of difficult tasks. For example, the failing schools had to be closed in ways that minimized disruption in the education of students attending them and that helped the affected families feel hopeful rather than demoralized. Moreover, appropriate designs had to be chosen for the condo schools, and the students from the closed schools and their families had to be helped to choose wisely among the alternatives. This is a city used to neighborhood high schools and unused to an educational "marketplace." However, the superintendent promised "a variety of models and strategies," and the mayor promised that "the specialized focus of a small high school will better engage young teenagers." Both explicitly said they wanted difference. They said they wanted to do more than distribute the students and teachers from the failing schools into a set of identical "houses." That had been tried in this city at least once before, without much benefit.

To undertake these politically difficult tasks, the district opened the Office of Small High Schools. The office was charged with investigating design options and with inviting selected designers to bring their designs to the city on a 5-year contract. The charge was a huge departure from ordinary business here. This is a city used to designing its own reforms and used to exercising tight and continuous central control. The Office of Small High Schools was also charged with supporting the designers in their efforts to fit the designs to the city and to the large school buildings they would share with others.

## Building Relationships

When Janelle Greene began laying the groundwork for her BP condo school within the former Buckeye High School building, her mind was focused especially on staff and student recruitment, on LTI prospects in the city generally and the neighborhood in particular, and on figuring out how to operate on the city's relatively low per-pupil expenditure. This was during what BP calls the TYBO year (for The Year Before Opening). By the end of her first year as principal, however, Greene told us that she wished that during TYBO she had placed more emphasis on "building relationships." To us, her phrase signifies the set of unanticipated political negotiations she faced over the course of her school's first year. All of them were consequences of the mayor's promise to move fast.

Greene's school, called the Buckeye Met, shares the four-story Buckeye Multiplex (including its cafeteria, library, gym, and other common spaces) with two other schools: a K–5 and a middle school. Politically, Greene told us, the neighborhood surrounding Buckeye is "in the throes of gentrification," and she believes that the designs for the three schools were chosen with this in mind—to appeal to different social class interests. Of course, negotiating social class differences between neighbors within a single educational building can be as difficult as doing the same within a single residential community (Gootman, 2004). For example, Buckeye Met's middle school neighbor is a school that emphasizes a highly structured curriculum and strict behavioral guidelines. The contrast with Buckeye Met's emphasis on individualized programs and projects and on learning in the community seems stark within what Greene calls the "crunch of shared space." This other school's principal asked Greene to maintain "greater control" over the Met students within the common space. For example, she objected to their "clustered way of walking to the cafeteria." Greene countered with an explanation that while the BP philosophy urges students to adapt their behaviors to the different demands of different environments, it also respects them as individuals learning to function as adults in the world. "They can't learn how to interact in a mixed environment if we structure it so much that they have no practice."

Meanwhile, difference has required political negotiation with parties outside the building too. The local City Council member, Greene told us, "is very leery of the Buckeye Met, because she doesn't want a bunch of European people, as she would say, coming in and practicing their new-wave ideas on poor African American students." And this councilperson is very important in the neighborhood: "like your minipresident, your area president for several neighborhoods."

The fact that Greene is herself African American has sensitized her to the councilperson's challenge, she told us, and may also have caused this potentially powerful critic to speak privately before going public with her criticism. "But she jumped on me," Greene explained, "when I said kids needed to do projects that help the community. She said, 'How are they going to help the community? They can't help the community, they have enough problems. There is too much on a child to think they are carrying the community on their shoulders.'"

"But I didn't mean it that way at all," Greene told us, "so I had to quickly try to help her understand. It is a give-back to the community. I don't just take from my community, but I take and I have something to give, and it doesn't have to be in a big way."

Did she understand? we asked. "No," Greene answered. "She left not understanding, even though I explained it at least two different ways." But Greene resolved to follow up, to invite the woman to student exhibitions and other school events as the Buckeye Met evolves. "You have to kind of watch her," Greene said, letting the councilperson stand in for a large variety of stakeholders. "You have to keep explaining."

Nor did the local councilperson prove to be the only individual outside the building to whom Greene needed continually to explain her school and with whom she needed to negotiate a welcome for the school's differences. Despite the superintendent's invitation of difference, and the mayor's espoused confidence in the educational power of difference, Greene found herself during the school's 1st year continually negotiating difference with many school district officials. These included some assigned to the Office of Small High School Development.

## A Matter of Curriculum

One point of contention with the district involved its commitment to a literacy curriculum for all high school students. This curriculum predated the small high schools initiative by about 6 months, both pitched as efforts to improve high schools. The district imported the curriculum from another city, where it had reportedly been effective in boosting adolescents' reading and writing skills and in improving their reading and other test scores.

"I thought BP had made it clear," Greene told us, "that this is not the kind of school that has content specialty. But now the system is saying, 'Oh, my God, these kids haven't been given the opportunity to develop their literacy. They need the Reading and Writing Power course.' Where is the word *course* even coming from? The Big Picture design doesn't include courses."

Greene felt that the district had exceeded the bounds of what she took to be its agreement with BP when it appointed a literacy teacher for Buckeye Met. But she decided to yield on the point. "The literacy teacher is working out," she told us later. "The good news is that she is flexible." Once hired, the teacher sensibly accepted Greene as her principal, and the two negotiated an understanding. On the one hand, they decided, the district needs a certain level of curricular compliance on literacy, and the literacy teacher has to satisfy her district supervisor that she is indeed a literacy teacher. On the other hand, Greene needs to stay faithful to BP principles, not least because visitors from the BP network will expect as much. "The literacy teacher is doing *that* part," Green told us, referring to several elements of the Reading and Writing Power course, "and then afterwards she is connecting with the project work that the students are doing. So that's not a bad thing."

What Greene feels *is* a bad thing, however, is the attention that the district tends to pay to only certain content areas, especially literacy and math. "I know where the push is," she says, referring to federal and state testing requirements. Yet in the year-end review of the school's outcomes, "they didn't even raise an eyebrow about social studies. It never came up. People will say to you that they don't just care about only reading and math, but if that is all you ever talk about, then I know that is all you care about." For Greene, "social studies" is not the traditional content area of the high school curriculum. It refers to a relationship between her students and the larger social environment that is at the heart of the BP curriculum. This is the difference that her school is all about, as far as Greene is concerned, and what disturbs her is the fact that it is not among the differences that the district seems to take note of.

Meanwhile, her larger concern is that this district that seems to invite difference may have little real appreciation of it. A small school here is considered equivalent to every other small school here. Smallness matters, but not the ideas that invest *this* way of being small as distinct from *that* way of being small. In such circumstances, Greene wonders, can she find sufficient support for the school to continue its political negotiations? "The system really doesn't know what to do with us," Greene told us. "They really don't. They don't understand what type of supports we need, what type of leadership we need, what type of time line we need. They don't know."

## Commentary

The benefit of using what Lee Bolman and Terry Deal (1997) call the "political frame"—deliberately highlighting the politics of a particular change situation while holding other dimensions at bay—is that it not only helps you see more clearly the conflicts you need to manage, but also helps you understand that conflict is a routine part of making change. Indeed, conflict is the evidence that change is actually happening. It's not *trouble* unless you don't see it and manage it. We think the conflict in this first case stems substantially from what Schön and McDonald (1998) call the predictable disconnection between intention, design, and practice. It occurs in any kind of complex change. This city is busy tampering with key elements of 20th-century public schooling—introducing school design contractors, giving the mayor and City Council substantial authority, encouraging an educational "marketplace," distinguishing between a school and a school *building*, and more. However, key people are not behaving as the advocates of these changes intend they should, and mechanisms to support the changes have in many cases not yet been invented or put in place. This makes for ambiguity and conflict. Moreover, as new designs and practices are introduced, old ones are not necessarily removed or altered. That's because the politics of addition is much easier than the politics of subtraction. The result is that the latest innovations have to jostle for room among sometimes incongruent predecessors.

Reading the case, our dialogue partner Howard Wollner sees a dilemma of "multiple masters," he tells us, and says it's common in the business world too. "At Starbucks, it happens when competing functions vie for the limited real estate that is the store footprint. Each believes that its offering deserves prime space." The resulting tensions can become quite heated, he adds, and he thinks the only way to resolve them is "to get back to seeing the store as an organic whole." In explaining what he means, he mentions the recent Starbucks effort, discussed in Chapter 1, to recapture its original appeal. "Should it eliminate hot breakfast sandwiches?" he asks. "It's a strong revenue and profit generator, but it is also a product that competes in the store with the smell of coffee." In resuming his role as CEO, Howard Schultz initially said that he would eliminate the breakfast sandwiches. In fact, however, he relented. "The breakfast sandwiches are staying," Wollner reports. "The profit was too great to walk away from—though they reformulated the cheese component to cut down the aroma in the store." Conflicts between multiple masters get resolved in many ways.

What is elemental to a BP school in Greene's view is its courseless design—the centrality of internship, project, and advisory—and the different kind of "social study" this design promotes. Greene clearly means to protect this. At the same time, she's practical about the politics. Although the case ends with a kind of sigh on her part, one that every reformer can relate to, it seems merely a pause. She will be calling up the councilperson to come over again for a chat.

Reading this first case, as well as the two others to follow, our other dialogue partner, Greg Farrell, realized a difference between the challenge of managing the politics of local adoption as BP experienced it early on, and as ELS did. "There are advantages and disadvantages to both beginnings," he says. But he adds that when he visits with other Gates grantees, he feels like a "genuine sophomore," because of the prior and different experience he had in New American Schools. He explains:

> You see, ELS didn't begin with a prototype. It wasn't one school that we built initially, but 10 schools at different demonstration sites through the New American Schools planning year. We didn't have the advantage of working it all out in some place like Providence until we got it mostly the way we wanted it. Without the benefit of a prototype, we got plunged into the context business fast: 10 schools, five cities. We had the somewhat more half-baked experience of seeing *some* of our vision implemented here and there, and then imagining how other parts might be. On the other hand, we also had the opportunity to learn all at once from 10 different locations. You see the same issue dealt with and received in so many different ways that you begin to understand what the issue *is*. Then you try to deal with that.

In the end, he concludes, "it was fortunate we learned the politics all at once." They thus became a source of design insight instead of a fidelity threat.

## CAUGHT IN THE MIDDLE

The Delmanto School District serves 50,000 students, K–12, who live in a sprawling city of a western state. Despite low per pupil expenditures in Delmanto—lower, in fact, than BP regards as the necessary threshold for proper funding of a Big Picture school—the district was one of the first sites that BP "prospected." One reason was that Dennis Littky and Elliot Washor had a relationship with then Superintendent of Schools Willy Grant, who told them that he wanted to "shake up" the city's high schools. Another reason was that Grant had secured external funding to do the shaking up. Without knowing much about the design itself, but trusting the designers and attracted to their idea about student passion as the driver of secondary education, Grant committed to opening two BP schools as district-operated charter schools.

Meanwhile, Grant also committed to turning the city's most notoriously failing high school, Delmanto Central High School, into six new schools-within-a-school. Here too he planned to use a charter design, though not a district-operated one. He planned to grant the charter to a not-for-profit and faith-based youth development effort called Hope Inc. The founder and funder of Hope Inc., George Moffat, is a charismatic graduate of Delmanto Central, who went on to make a fortune as a music producer, then moved back to his old neighborhood to help others gain choices. Hope Inc. sponsors many activities for youth, including sports clubs, summer camps, and neighborhood after-school centers.

The use of charters as a reform tool is among the practices that continually put Superintendent Grant at odds with the city's teachers union, and the ensuing labor problems are among the reasons that he and the school board decided to part ways with an early retirement agreement. This happened at about the same time that Jane Houseman was chosen to be the principal of the Delmanto Big Picture School. The district had initially put forward another candidate for the job, but BP found him unsuitable. It offered to recruit a substitute and found Houseman in Chicago. She was teaching in a successful charter high school there, eager to help start a new one, and willing to relocate more than 1,000 miles to a very different place.

By the time Houseman arrived in Delmanto prepared to scout LTI locations, woo parents and students, and learn a new politics, Houseman found Grant gone and the new superintendent, Grace Smith, just getting acquainted with the high school reform plan she had inherited from her predecessor. Houseman also found herself working with two men whose views of her school-to-be differed considerably. Jake Cooley, director of small schools, viewed it as one in a portfolio of unique and entrepreneurial schools requiring light-handed support. Gerry Rigby, deputy superintendent and administrator of small high school development grants from two large foundations, saw it as a particularly odd, if nonetheless full, member of the larger class of district secondary schools requiring strong district oversight. In effect, these two men represented different poles of a tension that Houseman felt acutely. It had to do with her school's ambiguous status. Of course, during her planning year, the school was still no more than a concept. But even as a concept, it was neither "regular," nor wholly irregular. It was a *district charter*, a phrase whose words seemed to cancel each other out. Cooley represented the *charter* side of the phrase, and Rigby the *district* side.

When we spoke with Houseman near the end of the Delmanto Big Picture School's 1st year of operation, she reflected on its beginnings through the prism of its ambiguous status. Being a district charter, she said, means functioning within two systems of oversight, one concerned with charter policies, the other with district policies. Each generates paperwork and management meetings. "It means," she added, "that negotiation happens every day, every hour. It means constant attempts to build good relationships." And these relationships must be built in the face of the fact that "the district hasn't figured out what to do with us."

Early on, Houseman decided to rely on Cooley as the school's "ombudsman"—though his somewhat contentious relationship with Rigby ensured that some number of his interventions would prove inconclusive at best. Houseman's choice signified an identification with the *charter* side of the *district charter* label. The choice likely reflected her background as a charter school principal, but it no doubt represented as well her calculation that the district (which had so quickly dispatched the superintendent who hired her) remained politically unstable and that in this situation, independence might be best for her school. Still, Houseman played up the *district* side of her school's status on occasion too. For example, she relished a good visit from Superintendent Smith. "The new superintendent loves us now," Houseman told us, following one visit. "She did a walk-through and was pleased. There is a sense of welcome here, and the superintendent got that when she came in the door."

## Charter Politics

One of the first things that Houseman had to do upon her arrival in Delmanto was to find a building to house her planned school. She found herself attracted to the Rocky Mount neighborhood of the city. It is a tough and gritty place, beset by gangs and drugs, but also spirited; multiracial and multiethnic; and in Houseman's judgment, hopeful. Moreover, it has relatively good public transportation lines, an important asset in a BP school site. Rocky Mount also happens to be the neighborhood where George Moffat lives, where most of his Hope Inc. youth programs are based, and where he and his colleagues were then busy transforming the failing Delmanto Central High School into a charter school of six schools-within-a-school.

At first it looked as if the new BP school would occupy space on the campus of Rocky Mount Community College. Indeed, Deputy Superintendent Rigby had made a "handshake deal" with the college president to house the new school there at a nominal rent. But the deal unraveled when the faculty senate balked at giving up the space. Houseman sensed that something was up when her Community College connections simply stopped communicating with her—just when she was in the middle of trying to recruit the new school's first students, and of course answering parents' and students' questions about where the new school would be located.

By then, Houseman had done a lot of networking in the city, following Dennis Littky's and Elliot Washor's advice to connect for the unforeseen resource benefits that connections can bring. She had met Moffat early on and cultivated a relationship. She knew that he was influential at City Hall, connected with the city's business community and the corporate community beyond, and well regarded by the city's African American community and by faith-based and other community activists.

Houseman also knew that she and he would inevitably come to be associated in people's minds just because they were both involved in high school development and charter schooling. Thus she needed to have a good sense of the man and his plans. This sense might prove helpful if she found herself having to head off a perception by the teachers union, for example, that her school was planning, like his, to open as a non-union charter school. She also thought that his perspective on what it means to be a charter school might be helpful to her as she began the task of negotiating her own school's charter status. She had heard that his negotiations with the district had been contentious and protracted.

For his part, Moffat sensed a possible advantage in connecting with his lesser-known colleague in new school design. When he heard that she had lost her school site at the community college, he offered an alternative site. He owned a small building that Hope Inc. had been using for an after-school program. But it was vacant now, the program having recently relocated to the elementary school that most of its participants attended. Would Houseman be interested in taking over the vacant site? He could give the district a free lease on the building for 2 years. By the end of the lease, her school would likely have grown out of the space, but she would have had the 2 years to search for a permanent home. For Houseman, the deal seemed irresistible, but the district took a long time to come around. At the time it was still negotiating with Moffat on the details of his charter at Delmanto Central.

When we first visited Houseman's school in its 1st year of operation, we had difficulty figuring out where to go. The only name on the building at the address we were given was "Hope Inc." Later, we learned, however, that the lease on the building had not after all gone to the district free of charge, but at what seemed to Houseman a hefty $80,000 a year. By the time the district responded to Moffat's original offer, he had changed his mind. But by then it was too late to find another site.

## Playing the Charter Card

When Houseman began to negotiate the terms of her own school's charter, she felt in an odd position. Here she was a new district administrator, hired by the suddenly retired superintendent, Willy Grant. Her job was to start a school that Grant had hoped would "shake up" the city's other schools. Now there was a new superintendent, Grace Smith, and Houseman was expected to negotiate with her the terms by which all of this might unfold—or not. What if Smith did not choose to start her term by trying to "shake up" other schools? This might be a sensible political move given her predecessor's fate. Of course, there were the foundation grants to consider. These had been given to the district to support charter conversion, and they obviously required follow-through. But Smith might be able to follow through in a different way from how her predecessor would have.

Still, Houseman continued to turn the dial deliberately toward the charter side of her school's identity. Drawing on her experience teaching in a charter school, she embraced the task of negotiating her new school's charter by accounting for the "freedoms" that she felt made her former school successful. Then she developed a strategy with one of the other district charter principals to persuade the district and the teachers union to grant these "freedoms." The strategy involved making serious plans to become independent charter schools, with a 501c parent organization as fiscal agent. They assumed that both the district and the union wanted them to stay district schools, but would not cede much regulatory authority without their strong threat to walk. At the 11th hour, they got most of what they wanted: (1) freedom to diverge from the district's scheduling system and calendar, though the schools are still constrained by state policies with respect to instructional days; (2) budgeting and spending freedom, within the fixed state allotment for charter schools; (3) freedom from the "bumping" provision of the district's collective bargaining agreement, protecting the district charter teachers from senior teachers elsewhere in the district who might choose to transfer in; (4) curriculum and instructional freedom, as consistent with the schools' designs; and (5) freedom to appoint their own advisory boards.

Houseman made sure that her advisory board was loaded with community clout. She wanted to ensure that it functioned as a de facto board of directors. Its members include a policy analyst at an important nearby educational think tank, who brings fiscal skills to the board; the CEO of LEAD (Linking Education and Academic Development) Delmanto, who happens to be a major connector in the city; a former Delmanto principal and director of personnel, whom Houseman called "my principal coach"; the head of a law firm, who practices education law and "does a lot of union grievance stuff," as Houseman put it; the associate editor of a business journal, who has been helpful in grant-writing; the development officer of a social service not-for-profit, who Houseman said "helps me think about how to use my board members well"; and the former provost of a state college, who has encouraged Houseman to "figure out how to translate what you do into the [state college] admissions system."

Now Houseman is looking for space again. The Hope Inc. building is inadequate in certain respects, particularly relative to its cost. In advance of Houseman's first meeting on the subject with Superintendent Smith, her board told her, "Say these words: 'The advisory board believes that Delmanto Big Picture School needs a permanent home, whether in an elementary school, or on its own.'" Sometimes in politics—as in learning and marriage—it is useful when someone tells you, "Say these words," to say them. So it proved in this case. Houseman said exactly these words, "and when she did," by Houseman's own account, "the superintendent went to her computer and e-mailed the district CFO: 'Why does Houseman not have a site yet?'"

## Commentary

New schools inherit the confusions of the place where they are located, which derive in part from the contradictions embedded in local reform history, and between one person's interpretation of this history and another's. But opportunity arises in the face of these confusions—if you expect it, can see it, and dare to act on it. The opportunity arises from a thicket of possible political affiliations. By *affiliation,* we mean a consciously political association, one intended to add power through a relationship. Of course, some affiliations are potentially advantageous, others potentially dangerous, and it is difficult to distinguish one from the other in advance. But politics is always about leverage, and new schools negotiating the politics of local adoption have to figure out where they can gain some. Affiliation of any kind is promising in this regard. The rest is all principled (or unprincipled) maneuvering.

For our dialogue partner Howard Wollner, this case study illustrates "how what may appear to be a solid plan can suddenly shift underneath your feet and require rapid response to the new dynamics." It happens all the time in business, he says, and "requires a quick assessment of the new landscape and gut decisions about how best to proceed." The heart of the challenge, he adds, is to "accept the change as inevitable, but attempt to retain those elements that are critical to the original concept and its perceived or known benefits." How best to do this? Houseman seems to have it down: "Building coalitions; seeking advocates; and most importantly, leading through influence rather than authority are highly effective ways of navigating such dynamic environments."

Our other dialogue partner, Greg Farrell, agrees, and adds that "one of the arenas where Big Picture is impressive is in the attention it pays to principals—selection, training, and support." Farrell thinks that the case also illustrates the mysterious ways in which the politics of local adoption intersect with the unique personal paths followed by the people who find themselves negotiating these politics. A long-standing axiom of politics is that it hinges on the personal. Farrell is mindful in this regard of Dennis Littky's path through Wading River and Winchester and how it honed his political sense. He mentions his own experience too:

> I took an Outward Bound [OB] course in 1963. I'd been a high school English teacher and a newspaper reporter. And I thought, couldn't you teach algebra like this? Couldn't you teach writing and reading like this? That's how I ended up starting an urban OB school. The local high school was willing to give us a couple hundred students from the general track. I got money from the Ford Foundation and the U.S. Office of Education. Outward Bound helped us too. We called the program Action Bound. This was in 1965. I hired a bunch of guys, including an OB instructor from England. We just made stuff up for these kids. Despite the fact that we didn't have the foggiest idea what we were doing, we were lively, we were doing cool stuff: 200-mile bicycle trips, lifeguarding on the Delaware River. A lot of the kids went to college. There were lots of little success stories. The problem was that I didn't realize then that when you start something so odd, you really should stay for a decade or it's going to get wiped out.

## INTERMEDIARY POLITICS

The southwest city we call Merton has a large Hispanic population with a 70% high school dropout rate. This statistic is an important background factor in the story that follows. Another important background factor is the state's participation in a private-public partnership for school reform, called Partners for Change, or just "Partners" for short. This late 1980s effort invested heavily in the professional development of teachers, relying for the most part on what experts today would call weak models of professional development, for example, after-school or daylong workshops taught by outside consultants, focused on topics not tightly tied to curriculum or instructional priorities. The apparent failure of Partners to make much difference, especially in reducing the achievement gap between White and Hispanic students, has assumed the status of an object lesson in the local political psyche. This is partly because Partners had a high profile, with the governor and a major foundation visibly involved, many dollars spent, and many teachers counted as participants. It is also because Partners and its sponsors invested little in evaluation and were therefore hard put to argue their own case. Finally, it is also partly because the decline of Partners coincided so neatly with the rise of a competing approach to school reform, one that eventually gained a lot of traction nationally, but got a head start here. By the mid-1990s, a policy consensus had emerged in this state concerning the value of integrating three strategies: the use of high-stakes assessments keyed to standards and curriculum frameworks; the encouragement of charter schooling and new school designs within the context of an "educational marketplace"; and outcomes-focused evaluation of schools, including measures disaggregated by race. More than a decade later, the wisdom of this approach seems a given to many reformers here, to an extent that is still rarer elsewhere.

BP was attracted to Merton because of one of the state's three strategic emphases, namely, the one concerned with chartering new school designs. In Jordan Nagle's view, however, BP overlooked the entanglement of this strategic emphasis with the other two. Nagle is the director of the Small Schools Project (SSP). Funded by grants from local as well as national foundations, SSP supports charter schools throughout the state. The support includes start-up assistance in the areas of charter application, fund-raising, hiring, and budgeting; and it also includes ongoing technical support in the form of leadership coaching, curriculum and instructional development, and formative evaluation.

Ironically, BP codirectors Dennis Littky and Elliot Washor had been introduced to Nagle years before by the executive director of Partners for Change. None of the three men were then enthusiasts of the Partners for Change approach. When Littky and Washor heard that Nagle was searching for good school designs to implement here, ones that particularly targeted students at risk of dropping out of high school, they got in touch. The result was that Nagle served as broker in BP's effort to get the Merton Public Schools to grant a charter to Desert Met, the state's first BP school and also one of SSP's client schools.

## A Challenging Debut

Both Nagle and the man hired to be the Desert Met's first principal, George Rhodes, recounted for us the details of BP's local political debut. Nagle told us that "the school board did not really want to deal with this—whether a Big Picture school should come to Merton. Basically their attitude was that we have our own problems and we're not into what you're into. In fact, the new superintendent's mandate was to be very streamlined in terms of curriculum, policy, et cetera. The last thing he wanted was some weird little school. But Merton was still willing to be charter friendly—has to be, because charters are popular politically. So it wouldn't be sabotage, it just wouldn't be supportive. But Big Picture didn't know much about all this."

For his part, Rhodes recalled the tough questions the board put to him. This was his first principalship, and he was new to school board politics. Meanwhile, he was also still getting used to the BP design. At one point, a board member asked him, "In the book [Eliot Levine's 2002 book about the Met], the Met collides head on with standards. In what ways do you collide?" It was, of course, a loaded question. At the time, Rhodes felt that some of the load might have been directed more at Nagle than at BP—a continuation of earlier battles between, on the one hand, one of the state's largest school boards and most reluctant grantor of charters, and, on the other, one of the state's most important charter enthusiasts. In any case, Rhodes felt nearly overwhelmed and was very grateful for the presence of Elliot Washor, who had flown in from Providence as a kind of expert witness.

But to Nagle's more politically tuned ears, the expert's testimony spelled trouble:

> Outsiders like Elliot would have no way to know this, but SSP had been hammering this city about the numbers. We'd been saying we need to see disaggregated cohort data. So when Elliot is an expert witness, and one member of the board asks whether the Desert Met kids will do well on the state assessment, and whether the kids will graduate and go on to college, Elliot said, "Absolutely." You have to understand that language is a hot-button issue around here. People have become savvy and conscientious about the language they use in talking about school effects. If you say that 100% of the kids stay in and go to college—and that's what Elliot implied—then people around here are going to be skeptical. "Really?" they'll say, "100%?"

Today, Washor recalls this meeting as a setup. "We were told that this was going to take 2 minutes, but it turned into an hour and the hour was televised. They really drilled us that day. I had to think very quickly."

## Managing Differences

In his SSP role, Nagle supports charter schools with many different school designs. All of them propose alternatives to mainstream public schools, he told us, but "some are like Starbucks, more easily inserted than others." BP is not among these. This is not a fault, he added. BP is a fine design, he said, but it needs more on-the-ground help to grow. One of the things that

SSP does, as an intermediary organization, is what Nagle calls "*translation*—for school board members, funders, and others." For example, SSP is now experienced, Nagle says, in explaining to people in Merton and elsewhere in the state that what others call classes, BP schools "call advisories." Elliot Washor's instinct in his prospecting here had been, by contrast, to avoid what seemed to him too simple (and potentially dangerous) translation. It was an instinct in Nagle's view that got the design into unnecessary political trouble. At the least, it left members of the board unsatisfied. One said she still needed "more clarity."

In general, SSP's work derives from the consensus we mentioned above concerning strategies for school reform. Like many others who have practiced school reform in this state and elsewhere over the course of the past decade, Nagle is convinced of the utility of a three-pronged approach: standards and curriculum, marketplace, and evaluation. The approach has a strong rational appeal in this state and elsewhere: set strong expectations, provide flexibility for inventive schools to meet these expectations, then ensure that they do. The problem that Washor and Littky see with this approach is that it tends to ignore what they take to be the predictably rough but generally reliable unfolding of BP school development and also of BP kids' development. They think it tries to rush both. Suspend rational haste, they argue. But it is hard to argue against haste in the context of the 70% Hispanic dropout rate that Merton experiences and in the presence of a consensus that there is a rational process of school development that can work to reduce this substantially.

Tension between these outlooks was evident in the first formative evaluation report that SSP issued on Desert Met, at the end of the school's 2nd month of operation. The report acknowledged the grim statistics the school faced. Barely a third of its 62 new students had passed the state's qualifying exam for high school. The rest lacked the credits they needed to take the exam. Many had poor discipline records in their former schools, and several had attended school fewer than 40 days the previous year. Some were active in gangs. "Traditional school structures fail children like this," the report said, "which is why SSP has supported the Big Picture model here."

The report went on to note encouraging signs of attachment—exactly what BP looks for also in the early days of its schools and in the early development of all its schools' students. One student told the evaluator, "If you would like observe me for a while, you'd see I changed a lot. Because I do my work, and last year I didn't want to come to school and now I do." This is just the moment, from a BP perspective—2 months in, and lightly attached—when a hard-to-reach student, gingerly pressed by a skillful advisor, can confront what it is she really wants her "work" to be, and then go on to find the right life-changing LTI. But the report urged moving faster than this. What the school needs "now," it concluded, was to press faster to get all its kids into an LTI, and to align the LTIs with the state's standards and curriculum frameworks.

Desert Met's principal Rhodes worked to negotiate the differences between BP and SSP. One partner gave him a design, a curriculum, a network, and an inspirational rhetoric that seemed to work well among students who might otherwise have given up hope in school success. With its national profile and its memorandum of understanding, this first partner also helped him carve out some room for his school to be different. Meanwhile, the other partner provided a lifeline to funders, policymakers, and local community leaders. It gave him formative feedback, which, however out of sync in some respects with BP strategy, used the same criteria on which his school will be judged when it comes time to renew its charter. Moreover, grounded in local political sensibility, it kept him attentive to the real stakes: not just keeping his school alive, but ensuring that his students graduate with the skills and knowledge they need to improve their prospects in the world.

But sometimes Rhodes had to make tough choices between his partners' values and strategies. In such circumstances, Rhodes told us that he had concluded, "I have more at stake with SSP and less so with Big Picture." The result was a degree of curricular adaptation at Desert Met by the end of its 1st year that set it apart from other BP schools, including, for example, direct instruction in math skills and writing.

## Commentary

Many people have a stake in the successful local adoption of an imported school design. They include the school designers themselves (both Elliot Washor and George Rhodes in this last case), and the parents and students they ultimately aim to serve. But all three of our cases highlight other stakeholders too, such as government officials and nearby school leaders as in the first case, local district officials and charter holders as in the second case, and regional intermediaries as in this last case. All these people are naturally more expert on the local school environment than the school designers can possibly hope to be. Of course, environments vary in terms of whether they have a prevalent and coherent theory of action for school reform, but to the extent that they do, new school designers should expect that their work will be evaluated by its lights. This does not necessarily mean that the designers should conform to this prevailing theory of action. Sometimes an oppositional niche is best, particularly if the theory of action is not so coherent, or if the coalition holding it together is beginning to fray. However, designers need to understand the cost of not conforming. Meanwhile, local politics have nuances that can easily elude an outside designer. For these two reasons especially, designers cannot successfully operate alone on the politics of local adoption. To gain the multiple levels of nuanced local knowledge that they need, the school designers need local partners, whether formal or informal. As the cases also suggest, having local partners adds yet another level of local politics to deal with, but the value may well exceed the cost.

This is true, Howard Wollner tells us, if the partners are the right ones. Indeed, he thinks all the stories in this chapter on the Political Challenge implicitly reflect another challenge altogether, what he calls the challenge of collaborating with other organizations. He thinks, for example, that the collaborating organization in the last case—SSP—"did not fully embrace or understand the game-changing nature of the Big Picture design." He draws an analogy between BP's entry into new and strange regions and districts and Starbucks's entry into foreign markets. There the Starbucks international business plan called for partners to "assume responsibility for all aspects of the Starbucks business in that country, with Starbucks providing guidance and product." When the selection of market partners was "thorough and carefully calibrated," Wollner says, "the markets proved very successful." But, he adds, when partners who were otherwise strong "did not possess a clear understanding and embrace of the 'Starbucks Experience,' the partnership often failed." This made business precarious because Starbucks had to do more than it bargained for, namely, run the market as a company-owned business, "which sometimes stretched Starbucks resources very thin."

# 6

# The Mindset Challenge

When we wrote the essays that informed this book, we counted seven challenges that BP faced as it scaled up its school design. But as we worked on the book, we found an eighth one. It happened when a reader of an early draft of the book asked us to account for the actual impact of BP schools on students' learning. "I understand," this reader said, "that your main purpose is to account for challenges and strategies going to scale, but other readers will want to know whether going to scale in this case has helped more kids. You've got to answer that question."

We do answer it here. We answer it first in one word and then in a few thousand more. The one word is *yes*. The few thousand more offer evidence for this *yes*, and also explore the challenge that underlies the question. This eighth challenge has to do with the difference that difference makes in school design. The further a design strays from traditional expectations about what school is and how it works, the more it incurs a penalty for being different. This is a deeply ironic challenge when difference is needed. And when it comes to high schooling in the United States, we are hardly alone in thinking that difference *is* needed. So challenge 8 presents a double bind. On the one hand, it spurs us to make radical change in the outcomes of American high schooling, such that everyone graduates and is prepared for higher education and an intellectually demanding workplace. On the other hand, it warns us against tampering too much with ordinary high school design in order to achieve this radical change in outcomes.

Just as we have our private names for earlier chapters—the olive oil chapter, the ice cream chapter—we've got one for this chapter too. This is our manifesto chapter. Analysis and analogy seem to us sufficient in exploring challenges 1 through 7, but we think protest is called for here. That's because the other challenges arise naturally, while this one is manufactured. We might more easily be able to dispense with it—hard as it is to change mindset—if we could see more clearly the harm it inflicts. One of the functions of protest is to make harm visible. Another is to spur collective action. School designers have to be the principal actors when it comes to meeting the other challenges, but all the rest of us have to pitch in to manage the Mindset Challenge. That's because it arises from public policy.

As manifestos go, however, ours may seem an odd one rhetorically. It begins with references to a film review in the *Washington Post*, goes on to explore (very briefly) the history of the American high school—which is also the history of the double bind—then looks closely at data on BP school outcomes. This is where the double bind becomes most visible. Finally, the chapter concludes with ideas drawn from a speech given by a distinguished psychometrician, or testing expert, to the American Educational Research Association annual meeting. Film reviews, history, numbers, psychometric research: hardly the stuff of radical rhetoric, you may think. And while our message *is* radical, part of our protest is with the fact that anyone would think so. Here is the message simply put: Let's give ourselves a chance to do what we say we want to do, namely, provide all youth an intellectually powerful high schooling.

Challenges of mindset require unlearning, as two of our favorite deep thinkers suggest. One is the philosopher Nel Noddings, who asks us with regard to this particular challenge of mindset to unlearn the ways we approach goal-setting in education. Give up, she writes, the single ideal of the educated person, and replace it with multiple models "to accommodate the multiple capacities and interests of students" (1992, p. 173). Where do such "models" come from? The historian and education reformer Ted Sizer (2004) says that they are all around us if we will only unlearn our habit of thinking about education solely in terms of schools. Replace schoolcentric accountability, he advises, with one that focuses as well on larger social influences.

## WHAT WE THINK ABOUT WHEN WE THINK ABOUT HIGH SCHOOL

From the *Washington Post*:

> We're stuck in the library in Shermer, Ill. Mr. Vernon pops in every half-hour to bark at us, set us straight. We're still a brain, a beauty, a jock, a rebel and a recluse, and we're not allowed to talk ourselves out of it. We glance at the clock. Half past 2008. We've been here for 23 years, since "The Breakfast Club." . . . We're still trying to figure out, first, who we are, and . . . who the high-schoolers of today are. (Zak, 2008, p. M1).

These are the opening lines of Dan Zak's review of *American Teen*, a documentary about high school that proved a hit at the 2008 Sundance Film Festival. The title of Zak's review caught our eyes: "Suspended in Time: Why Can't Hollywood Graduate to a *Bigger Picture* of High School Life?" (our italics). He accuses the film of complicity in a trap that Americans set for their youth. It is made of archetypes that disguise the real differences between youth and suggest that they are somehow on a different human plane from that of older people. On this other plane, they appear more limited than older people in the range and passion of their interests, less mature in their moral capacity and awareness, more inclined to act impulsively than deliberately, more prone to foolish than to wise behavior, less capable of producing spectacular work by any standard, more likely to act criminally. Our refusal to admit that they are actually quite *like* older people in all these categories, which is to say, variable, has dictated how we school them. Thus we typically separate them from the rest of society and its occupations. We make them form a society apart, a preparatory society. During their school hours we give them little opportunity to become deeply engaged in anything, as if they were only capable of superficial engagement, as if they did not need the kind of intense engagement that older people crave and benefit from, and that many young people cram into their out-of-school hours (Csikszentmihalyi & Schneider, 2000). Meanwhile, we severely constrain and monitor their society apart, using devices that range from lines and bells to metal detectors and police guards. We track them into groups based on archetypes and baseless estimations of their future; rarely afford them the learning advantage of crossing group lines; give them very little discretion over their time and movement; and censor their speech and other expression to a degree unthinkable in college, for example. The characters in *The Breakfast Club*, the 25-year-old film by John Hughes that Zak's review alludes to, spend most of the film in Saturday detention. But they manage there to bond across archetypes and famously conclude, "What we found out is that each one of us is a brain . . . an athlete . . . a basket case . . . a princess . . . and a criminal" (Zak, 2008, p. M10).

Of course, the film itself is a manifestation of one advantage that youth gain in the otherwise dangerous bargain that is the Breakfast Club high school. They become shapers of and participants in a powerful peer culture, one with its own economy, aesthetics, and educational impact (Rury, 2004). The BP design tries, on the one hand, to respect the power of this peer culture, while, on the other, ensure that it stays connected with a large swath of adult culture. This swath goes well beyond the kind of adult culture represented by Shermer High School's Mr. Vernon.

## HISTORY OF HIGH SCHOOLING

When the term *high school* was first used, in Boston, in the 1820s, it was still just an adjective modifying a common noun.* William Reese (1995) reports that "Americans throughout the early 1800's wrote approvingly of schools of a 'higher order' " (p. 34), though anything beyond the rudiments qualified as "higher order." Many designs thrived and competed. Town-supported Latin grammar schools emphasized the study of classical languages and texts and prepared students for college. Small entrepreneurial schools, advertising in broadsides or newspapers, offered training in such subjects as writing, navigation, and gunnery. Tuition-supported academies and seminaries offered some classical study too, but mostly emphasized subjects like bookkeeping, agriculture, needlework, surveying, or pedagogy (Reese, 1995; Sizer, 1964a, 1964b). There were also secondary departments of colleges, as well as colleges that combined what we would today call Grades 11 through 14 (Gleason, 1995). Finally, there were common schools that taught some number of older students the "higher branches," as well as "town schools" that reserved a top floor of their buildings for a "higher school."

Higher schooling proved popular in the 19th century for the same reason that "higher education" proved popular in the 20th, namely, economic change. The new market economy reached even inland villages and farms in the early 1800s, and advancing industrialization and labor organization as well as increasing immigration throughout the century disrupted established patterns of youth employment and apprenticeship (Labaree, 1988; Reese, 1995). In responding to these economic shifts, higher schooling supplemented the moral and political purposes of "lower" schooling. It focused on the development of human capital fit for a market economy and did so in a way (featuring multiple competing designs) that seemed compatible with this economy (Cohen & Neufeld, 1981; Krug, 1972; Labaree, 1988). Ordinary families sensed the advantage in this for their children, while elites promoted it as protection against class warfare, the latter being a continual danger amid the century's recurring panics and depressions and in the presence and aftermath of a bloody civil war (Reese, 1995). By the 1930s, however, American high schooling had evolved into *high school*, a noun phrase, denoting a standardized design and evoking an architectural image part factory and part cathedral. Nonetheless, attending a high school remained far from universal until the 1960s, and graduating from

---

*Much of the brief history that follows here is paraphrased from an essay published by one of the coauthors as a chapter in Floyd Hammack's *The Comprehensive High School Today* (McDonald, 2004).

one remains far from universal even today (Angus & Mirel, 1999; *Education Week*, 2008; Reese, 1995).

We briefly recount below the history of this institution—this *high school*—emphasizing both its shapers and its resistors. As you might imagine, BP schooling has roots in the resistance. The shapers generally imagined a standardized and perfectible institution, growing each decade to enroll eventually all youth, while the resistors—with an eye on the diversity among all youth—invented alternative institutions.

## Some Shapers of the High School

Notable among the shapers of the high school was the Committee of Ten, a group of influential educators appointed by the National Education Association (NEA) in 1892 and led by the president of Harvard University, Charles W. Eliot. They aimed to clean up the institutional messiness they perceived in 19th-century secondary schooling. In the 1890s, modernization was often equated with institutional uniformity (Krug, 1964). The committee prescribed five curricular "main lines" for the high school curriculum: courses in English, mathematics, science, history, and foreign languages. These were to be packaged into classes lasting a little less than an hour each day. This prescription established the structure and schedule of the high school as it typically remains nearly 130 years later (Sizer, 1986). However, the committee proved less influential (at least for about 120 years) with regard to another of its design recommendations. It was against incorporating vocational or commercial study into the high school. It wanted the high school to focus exclusively on the collegiate disciplines, and it argued that these would benefit all students, including those not preparing for college. This argument explicitly staked out the double bind: benefit all students, *but* stick to the collegiate disciplines. For the rest of the century, the shapers of the high school would alternately resist and embrace this formulation, even as they made the institution itself ubiquitous and nearly universal.

In 1918, for example, another NEA committee issued a report that rejected the idea of a collegiate curriculum for all, but otherwise kept the idea of a universal high school design intact. It was in the *Cardinal Principles of Secondary Education* that the term *comprehensive high school* was coined (U.S. Bureau of Education, 1918). This institution would educate all youth, but within a differentiated curriculum—leveled for different abilities and educational aims and expanded to include subjects like health, leisure, citizenship, and what the committee called "worthy home-membership." The large influence of the *Cardinal Principles* coincided with the emergence of the new technology of intelligence testing, which promised an efficient sorting of those students for whom worthy home-membership seemed more important than algebra or Latin. The *Cardinal Principles* imagined a crossroads institution like the one *The Breakfast Club* portrayed many years later, where in 1983 terms, geeks, greasers, and prin-cesses on different life paths occasionally meet in homeroom, assemblies, or detention. "Life in such a school," the report declared, "is a natural and valuable preparation for life in a democracy" (p. 20).

The midcentury champion of the comprehensive high school James B. Conant also viewed the institution as a contributor to democracy, even a guarantor of it (Conant, 1960; Hammack, 2004). Like Eliot, he was a Harvard president, though a former one by the time he became a high school reformer. He was then fresh from a stint as U.S. high commissioner in occupied Germany. In 1959, following extensive visits to high schools throughout the United States, Conant wrote a book, called *The American High School Today*, assessing the conditions of these schools. He made some recommendations for change that proved very influential. In particular, he deplored the fact that more than 70% of high schools then had fewer than 100 students in the 12th grade. He thought this made them too small to be truly comprehensive in their offerings, particularly with respect to the needs of the academically "gifted." He recommended consolidation, calling for a reduction from 21,000 high schools to 9,000. Today, there are roughly 16,000 high schools in the United States, though these enroll at least 60% more students than in 1960 (Digest of Educational Statistics, 2000; U.S. Census Bureau, 1960). Conant's prescription to make high schools bigger arrived just in time to accommodate postwar baby boomers either as sub-urban adolescents or as racially redlined urban adolescents.

By the 1980s, the big comprehensive high school was well established throughout the United States, though the impact of racial segregation made it far less the contributor to democracy than Conant had projected. More-over, the emerging knowledge economy—and what we would later call globalization, with its flight of blue-collar jobs from the United States—eroded its economic rationale as well. In other words, by the mid-1980s, sorting students into stronger and weaker intellectual "tracks" was begin-ning to seem disadvantageous from a national policy perspective, even if many families still regard it as socially advantageous. *A Nation at Risk*, the widely read 1983 report of the National Commission on Excellence in Edu-cation, did not dismiss sorting, but in doomsday prose it did insist on a general lifting of intellectual expectation in high schooling. The report's second paragraph begins, "If an unfriendly foreign power had attempted to impose on America the mediocre educational performance that exists today, we might well have viewed it as an act of war." And the same para-graph concludes: "We have in effect been committing an act of unthinking,

unilateral educational disarmament" (p. 5). As is typical, however, of what
David Tyack and Larry Cuban (1995) call utopian reform documents, the
doomsday prose of *A Nation at Risk* switches quickly to a messianic one.
Thus near the end of its 36 pages, the report declares: "America can do it!
We are the inheritors of a past that gives us every reason to believe that we
will succeed" (p. 34).

Succeed at what? Well, nothing less than fixing the high school so that
it can in turn save the American economy. As we say, *A Nation at Risk* at-
tacked the intellectual flabbiness of the comprehensive high school, though
not its fundamental design. Its remedies included more required courses,
more homework, more testing, and explicit standards for student achievement. Over the next quarter-century, backed by vast amounts of state, federal, and foundation dollars, its recommendations in particular for more
testing and more explicit standards for student achievement proved hugely
influential. In the process, the high school was pressed to become more like
the kind of institution that the Committee of Ten had urged from the
beginning—not just more intellectually focused, but more academic. As we
will suggest below, there is a difference.

## Resisters Along the Way

Such formidable shapers of the high school as Eliot, the *Cardinal Principles*,
Conant, *A Nation at Risk*, and others too numerous to mention in this brief
account encountered resistors who encouraged more diversity in high
schooling. Among them were the planners of President Franklin Roosevelt's
New Deal, who tried to manage youth unemployment in the 1930s by challenging the high school's claim to be the chief custodian of youth (Krug,
1972; Tyack, Lowe, & Hansot, 1984). Two New Deal initiatives were involved. The first was the Civilian Conservation Corps, a very popular
forerunner of contemporary youth service projects. The CCC operated
residential camps for older youth (17–25) throughout the country. These
combined education with paid work on such conservation projects as for-
est reclamation, flood prevention, and park construction. Between 1933 and
1942, more than 2 million youth attended CCC camps (Krug, 1972). The
other New Deal high schooling project was the youth division of the Works
Progress Administration (WPA). Called the National Youth Administration (NYA), it began in 1935 as a source of part-time employment for high
school and college students from out-of-work families. Schools and colleges
designed the projects these students worked on—mostly construction and
repair projects—while the federal government paid the bill. By 1940, however, NYA also operated some 600 "resident centers" that enrolled some
30,000 youth. Paid for their efforts, the enrollees spent half their 8-hour days

in service work projects and the other half in education, including vocational instruction and related work in English, math, and social studies (Krug, 1972). Krug reports that these resident centers appeared to establishment educators "suspiciously like schools," and that for this reason the "schoolmen" tried to shut them down (p. 323). Indeed, both the NYA and the CCC did shut down fairly abruptly in the early 1940s, though their demise likely owed more to World War II and the draft than to the political maneuvering of the "schoolmen."

After the war, as we mentioned above, Conant's efforts to encourage bigger comprehensive high schools dovetailed influentially with the vast expansion of American metropolitan areas and new school construction. At the same time, however, these efforts eventually encountered resistance too, this time on moral and even aesthetic grounds. And again the resistance gained federal financing. It came from Title III of the Elementary and Secondary Education Act (ESEA), originally passed in 1964 and reauthorized many times afterward (and in 2001 renamed No Child Left Behind). In his best-selling 1970 book, *Crisis in the Classroom*, Charles Silberman captured the spirit of this particular wave of high school resistance:

> Because adults take the schools so much for granted, they fail to appreciate what grim, joyless places most American schools are, how oppressive and petty are the rules by which they are governed, how intellectually sterile and esthetically barren the atmosphere, what an appalling lack of civility obtains on the part of teachers and principals, what contempt they unconsciously display for children as children. (p. 10)

His voice was an establishment echo (by a respected journalist, funded by the Carnegie Corporation) of more radical critiques by Edgar Z. Friedenberg (1964, 1965), John Holt (1964), Paul Goodman (1964), Ivan Illich (1971), A. S. Neill (1960), and others. Their messages were abetted by a spate of muckraking books about actual schools, particularly urban ones, and also by books that offered images of alternative kinds of schooling, for example, Joseph Featherstone's (1971) *Schools Where Children Learn*, and at the high school level, John Bremer's and Michael von Moschzisker's (1971) *The School Without Walls*. Silberman writes that Bremer's Parkway Program in Philadelphia—a forerunner of BP schooling—was founded on the premise that the comprehensive high school had by 1970 "reached the end of its development" (Silberman, 1970, quoting Bremer, p. 349). Indeed, throughout the United States in these years, a number of *alternative* high schools opened, funded by ESEA Title III. In New York City, for example, dozens of such schools were created, some designed from scratch and some incorporating private "street academies" that had been launched earlier to accommodate youth and their families eager for an alternative to the city's large and often grim factory high schools (Phillips, 2000). Others in New York or elsewhere were modeled on "free schools," educational expressions of the hippie movement then waxing. All defined themselves in opposition to the comprehensive high school: They were smaller, looser, and countercultural. As Bremer suggested, these schools were not about reforming the high school, but about moving beyond it, even returning to a prior condition of diversity in secondary education. In New York at least, many of the alternative high schools survived, and multiplied—later serving as exemplars for the early-21st-century small high schools movement, funded in large measure by the Bill and Melinda Gates Foundation.

Influential as *A Nation at Risk* proved to be in the 1980s, it shared the reform stage with other influential perspectives on high school reform, including one that came to regard the conventional high school design as flawed beyond repair. Notable among reformers who advanced this idea is the education historian and reform activist Ted Sizer. Like Eliot and Conant, Sizer has Harvard roots (former dean of the Graduate School of Education), though significantly he also has experience as a high school principal (the job he went to *after* leaving the Harvard deanship). In the late 1970s/early 1980s, Sizer conducted a research project called the Study of the American High School. It yielded three books, whose titles alone suggest its overall findings: Arthur Powell's, Eleanor Farrar's, and David Cohen's (1985) *The Shopping Mall High School*; Robert Hampel's (1986) history of the high school, called *The Last Little Citadel*; and Sizer's own (1984) *Horace's Compromise: The Dilemma of the American High School.* The study concluded that the very design of the conventional high school was responsible for the intellectual shallowness and incoherence of its curriculum, for the impersonal and even alienating environment that so many of its students reported experiencing, and for the fact that high school teachers (like the composite character Horace Smith portrayed in Sizer's book) teach less powerfully than they would like and less effectively than their students deserve. In other words, the study found the conventional high school design seriously *im*perfectible. So while policy-oriented reformers set out to improve the design, especially through the introduction of curriculum standards and testing, Sizer and a band of school-based reformers who joined him in the Coalition of Essential Schools, including Dennis Littky, set out in increasingly bold moves through the 1980s and into the 1990s to restructure it. The coalition had no one design to offer in place of the conventional high school design, but rather a set of design principles. Notable among them are two that in juxtaposition acknowledge the double bind and call on designers to design their way out of it. The first principle urges reformers to figure out how to teach *all* students to use their minds well, and the second urges them to figure out how to take seriously the fact that these students differ from each other – not in the archetypal ways that *The Breakfast Club* and *American Teen* portray, but in the myriad ways that adults differ from each other too.

By the middle of the 1990s, Sizer and other reformers associated with the coalition had moved on from "restructuring" to the more fundamental kinds of design changes discussed in the opening section of this book. Sizer himself, for example, founded a novel and successful charter high school, the Francis W. Parker School, in Harvard, Massachusetts. He also founded the Annenberg Institute for School Reform, at Brown University, whose first fellows were Deborah Meier, then helping to formulate a plan to reconstitute all of the big high schools in New York City into small condo schools, each with its own design; Howard Fuller, then (as now) promoting vouchers as a way to provide school choice to poor urban families; and Dennis Littky, then busy with Elliot Washor dreaming up the Big Picture Company.

## BIG PICTURE ACCOUNTABILITY DATA: INSIDE THE DOUBLE BIND

In Chapter 1, we noted that the Bill and Melinda Gates Foundation classifies the new school designs it has supported in going to scale into three categories it calls *traditional*, *theme-based*, and *student-centered* (www .gatesfoundation.org). All three categories of design contribute to the different kind of high schooling we promote. Such difference in design, we think, makes for equity of opportunity, particularly for students who have for various reasons found the conventional 20th-century high school an uncomfortable fit. In particular, we think that the second and third categories of design in the Gates classification are valuable insofar as they challenge our mindset, not only about the culture of high school but also about its content. Thus one category-3 design—namely, BP's—does not follow the outline of the high school curriculum introduced in 1892 by the Committee of Ten. That is, it does not divide content into "subjects," time into "courses," and space into "classrooms." Within the BP design, content is channeled into broad intellectual constructs called Learning Goals: communication, empirical reasoning, social reasoning, quantitative reasoning, and character development. Time is split between LTIs and Advisory. And space is designed to accommodate project work, small-group work, exhibitions, visits by prospective mentors, and easy interaction with the community. When we first visited the Met sites explicitly built to be Met sites, we were struck by how difficult it would be to transform them into ordinary schools. The "classrooms" would be too small, the small nooks too plentiful, the overall space more like adult workspace than student work-space. Such differences of fundamental design matter. For most students, parents, and policymakers, they make BP schools seem vastly unlike any other schools they have known. For some of these people, this is a turnoff. For others, it is a godsend. In either case, as we said above, the difference presents a challenge that BP must wrestle with, one that manifests itself especially in the complex arena that in the early 21st century we have come to call *accountability*.

In what follows, we explore BP school effectiveness data from the perspectives of the Rhode Island and California state accountability systems, both heavily influenced by the federal law called No Child Left Behind. We use only Web-available data in this exploration and do not manipulate it any other way than to put it into what we regard as reasonable comparison sets. Our exploration has two purposes. First, we want to substantiate the "yes" we offered at the start of the chapter to the question of whether more students are likely to benefit as BP grows its network of schools. Second, we want to illustrate the double bind at the heart of the Mindset Challenge.

We focus on Rhode Island for the obvious reason that Rhode Island is the home of the Met—the original BP school, and still the one that has graduated the most students. Because most BP schools grow by adding one grade a year, few of the network's schools had graduated students by 2008 when this book went to press. It also happens that Rhode Island has an elaborate and fairly transparent accountability system that makes finding the right comparison group easier than in many other places. This is also true for California, which is the home of three of the first six schools outside Rhode Island to graduate students.

## Rhode Island

Rhode Island treats the Met (Metropolitan Career and Technical Center) as a single school for accountability purposes, though the Met functions for the most part as six separate BP schools. The single-school categorization may be misleading for some purposes, but it makes the data we are reporting more trustworthy inasmuch as it spreads random fluctuations across a bigger population. For an appropriate comparison group, we chose all the Providence public high schools—which include a mix of one academic exam school, several vocationally focused schools, several other small "themed" schools, and several large "comprehensive" high schools, 13 in all. (We have excluded from this count only the most recently opened high schools that have as of 2008 too little extant data to analyze.) Demographically, the Met has a higher proportion of White students than the

Providence high schools collectively do, but is roughly equal in terms of family income (See Table 6.1).

The Rhode Island Department of Education annually issues three sets of what it calls school report cards (Rhode Island Department of Education, 2007). This is likely confusing to some policymakers, parents, or others who might prefer one source of accountability information, even a single score as some accountability systems yield. We believe, however, that more information from multiple sources (within bounds, as Howard Wollner suggests in Chapter 5) is a good thing and leads to better judgments by those who need to weigh the information.

One of the Rhode Island report cards functions as the compliance vehicle for the federal education law No Child Left Behind (NCLB). To understand the information it yields, you need to know how NCLB works. That's complicated, so bear with us. NCLB requires that high school students be tested statewide in math and reading at least once during their high school years. The results must then be disaggregated and reported publicly in terms of subgroups based on race, English-language proficiency, disability status, and economic status. Rhode Island tests its high school students at the beginning of grade 11 using a testing program called the New England Common Assessment Program (NECAP), which it developed in collaboration with Vermont and New Hampshire. NCLB also requires that states set annual targets for test performance—rising incrementally from a baseline to full proficiency by 2014. Following federal guidelines, the Rhode Island targets rise from a 2002 baseline in 3-year steps through 2010, then jump every year thereafter to reach what NECAP defines as 100% proficiency in 2014. In 2007—the year we are reporting on here—Rhode Island was in the 3rd year of the first step above the baseline. This means that the 2008 results, based on targets scheduled to rise, are likely to put many more Rhode Island schools into NCLB jeopardy.

The policy jargon for NCLB jeopardy is "failing to make AYP" (for *adequate yearly progress*). This happens when a school misses the overall test

**Table 6.1.** Student demographics: comparing the Metropolitan Regional Career and Technical Center with other Providence public high schools

|  | Hispanic | African-American | White | Asian | Eligible for subsidized meals |
|---|---|---|---|---|---|
| The Met | 41% | 28% | 26% | 3% | 61% |
| Providence | 56% | 22% | 14% | 6% | 66% |

Source: Rhode Island Department of Education statistics, 2006–2007 (http://www.ride.ri.gov/)

score target (or percentage of students tested) in reading or math, or in any *one* of the subgroups in either reading or math, or (at the high school level) in the target graduation rate. This amounts to a whopping 37 targets in all. Missing just one equals failure to make AYP. Of course, a school may miss multiple targets, and urban high schools serving economically disadvantaged students often do. When a school misses one or more targets 2 years in a row, NCLB sanctions kick in. They start with relatively mild ones like having to notify all parents that they have a right under the law to ask for tutoring or a transfer, to the ultimate closing and reconstitution of the school. The way a school escapes escalating sanctions is to make AYP 2 years in a row.

Districts can also fail to make AYP. Under Rhode Island rules, this happens when the district has missed one or more targets at more than one school level (elementary, middle, or high), or if more than 40% of its schools have failed to make AYP. When a district (or school) has failed to make AYP for 2 years in a row, it is classified as being on "intervention status." In 2007, the Providence School District was in its 6th year of intervention status.

As we write this chapter, NCLB is under a cloud. Its initially strong political support has declined dramatically as more and more schools across the nation have failed to make AYP. The rate of failure is rising because the targets are rising. Support has waned also as the public has begun to recognize the distorting impact of NCLB's high-stakes-testing demands on what schools teach and on how much time they devote to test preparation (Darling-Hammond, 2007; Dillon, 2007; Hoff, 2007). Few dispute the value of NCLB in highlighting persistent school failure or persistent failure among subgroups within apparently successful schools. However, the bad side effects of the law are considerable. They include a faulty definition of proficiency, compounded by a mindless march toward perfect "proficiency" by 2014. (More about this below.) The bad side effects also include severe constraints on what can be done to remedy the failure that the spotlight on subgroups turns up. We are especially interested in these constraints because they affect how different a high school can afford to be—even, ironically, to address the needs of students left behind.

Table 6.2 compares Met 2007 Rhode Island NCLB Report Card statistics with those of all Providence high schools, as well as all high schools in Rhode Island. Note that the targets and report card scores are not percentages of students reaching proficiency. They are a derived measure called the Index Proficiency Score. This is calculated by the Rhode Island Department of Education based on the percentage of students scoring within each of the four NECAP proficiency bands, from substantially below proficient to proficient with distinction (Rhode Island Department of Education, 2007).

**Table 6.2.** NCLB Report Card statistics: comparing Metropolitan Regional Career and Technical Center with other Providence public high schools, and all public high schools in Rhode Island

| | Met | | Providence high schools | | All RI high schools | |
|---|---|---|---|---|---|---|
| | *English Language Arts (target: 68.8)* | *Math (target: 54)* | *English Language Arts (target: 68.8)* | *Math (target: 54)* | *English Language Arts (target: 68.8)* | *Math (target: 54)* |
| All students | 79.4 | 57.8 | 79.1 | 60.0 | 85.0 | 73.3 |
| African American | 79.3 | 55.0 | 79.0 | 56.5 | 79.1 | 59.2 |
| Asian | * | * | 81.9 | 68.0 | 87.1 | 76.9 |
| Hispanic | 77.3 | 56.3 | 77.7 | 58.1 | 77.5 | 58.8 |
| Native American | * | * | * | * | 76.4 | 59.3 |
| White | 84.2 | 66.3 | 84.3 | 70.1 | 87.3 | 77.7 |
| Students with disability | 71.9 | 50.2 | 63.4 | 41.1 | 69.2 | 50.0 |
| English language learners | * | * | 65.2 | 48.1 | 65.8 | 49.5 |
| Economically disadvantaged students | 77.8 | 55.3 | 78.7 | 58.8 | 78.4 | 61.4 |
| Graduation rate | 94.9 | | 82.1 | | 89.2 | |
| AYP status | Caution | | Intervention | | | |

* Indicates fewer than 45 students in this category which is the minimum for evaluation

*Source:* Rhode Island Department of Education Statistics, 2006–2007 (http://www.ride.ri.gov)

In the 2006–7 school year, based on an administration of the NECAP exams in March 2007, the Met made all but one of the NCLB targets, namely math scores for students with disabilities. It missed this target by 3.8 points. However, the mean score for all Rhode Island high schools fell short of the same target by 4.0 points, and the mean score for all Providence high schools missed it by 9.1 points. For missing this one target, the Met earned a "caution" status—a 1-year safe harbor for otherwise high- or moderately performing schools that miss up to three targets. The 13 individual Providence high schools varied in terms of making AYP (5 did and 8 did not, with the number of missed targets ranging from 10 to 23), and the district as a whole remains in intervention status. Meanwhile, the Met not only exceeded the graduation rate target, but came in just .1 short of the state's 2014 goal of 95%. This was 5.7 points ahead of the Rhode Island high schools overall, and 12.8 points ahead of the Providence high schools.

The second Rhode Island report card reports data directly from NECAP, namely, the percentage of students in each band of proficiency (Table 6.3). In doing so, it shifts the perspective away from the benchmarks—that is, hitting or missing this year's targets and making AYP *this* time. It highlights instead the distance to the 2014 targets, preset at 100% proficiency.

**Table 6.3.** NCLB reading and math proficiency levels achieved: comparing Metropolitan Regional Career and Technical Center with other Providence public high schools, and all public high schools in Rhode Island

| Reading | Proficient with Distinction | Proficient | Partially proficient | Substantially below proficient |
|---|---|---|---|---|
| Met | 4% | 34% | 48% | 14% |
| All Providence high schools | 8% | 36% | 31% | 24% |
| All RI high Schools | 16% | 45% | 24% | 14% |
| **Math** | *Proficient with Distinction* | *Proficient* | *Partially proficient* | *Substantially below proficient* |
| Met | 0% | 2% | 9% | 89% |
| All Providence high schools | 0% | 9% | 20% | 71% |
| All RI high schools | 1% | 21% | 27% | 51% |

*Source:* Rhode Island Department of Education Statistics, 2006–2007 (http://www.ride.ri.gov)

In the area of reading, the Met comes in 2% behind the Providence high schools in the "proficient" category. However, it has 10% fewer students in the "substantially below proficient" category, and 17% more in the "partially proficient" category. As formative feedback, this information seems a spur to making corrective adjustments with an eye to next year's higher NCLB target in reading and the 2014 goal. Moreover, it suggests that improving the reading proficiency of the substantial number of partially proficient 11th graders in time for their graduation is feasible, especially since we know that Met students tend to stay on and graduate (unlike many other high school students with reading difficulties). By contrast, the news in math seems quite discouraging for the Met: 89% of the eleventh graders "substantially below proficient." This seems, on the one hand, a call for major overhaul, even abandonment of the school's nontraditional approach to teaching math. On the other hand, the magnitude of the number combined with the weak showing of the comparison group also provokes questions about the test. A fundamental one from the perspective of the Met is this: What exactly is the proficiency this test measures such that the Met as designed misses it so nearly completely? Meanwhile, although the Providence high schools overall have 18% fewer students in the "substantially below category," they still have a whopping 71% there—hardly a strong endorsement of the traditional approach to teaching high school math that most of them follow. Moreover, when we look at the aggregate math scores for each of the 13 Providence high schools, we find that the exam school had a proficiency rate of 40%—double the state mean score and fifth highest in the state, though still surprisingly low for a population of students that by definition are good test takers. In the remaining Providence high schools, the math proficiency scores ranged from 0% to 9%, with a mean score of only 3%—which is 8% below the Met.

The third Rhode Island school report card draws data from Information Works, an ongoing collaboration of the Rhode Island Department of Education and the National Center on Public Education and Social Policy at the University of Rhode Island. It supplements student achievement data with administrative data on graduation, attendance, and school safety, as well as survey data obtained from parental, student, and teacher surveys. In Table 6.4, we present 2007 data on these indicators comparing the Met with the Providence High Schools and Rhode Island high schools overall (www.infoworks.ride.uri.edu).

## California

The California "accountability workbook" that the state had to prepare for federal inspection under NCLB derives principally from the 1999 state law called the Public Schools Accountability Act. It established a statewide

**Table 6.4.** Information Works: comparing Metropolitan Regional Career and Technical Center with other Providence public high schools, and all public high schools in Rhode Island on selected indicators

| Indicators | The Met | Providence high schools | Rhode Island high schools |
|---|---|---|---|
| Graduation rate | 94.9% | 82.1% | 89.2% |
| Attendance rate | 92.1% | 81.7% *(range: 55% to 100%, median: 78.7%)* | 90.4% |
| Percentage of students reporting that they can talk to a teacher or other staff member about personal or family problems | 52% | 17.8% | 17% |
| Percentage of students reporting that they can talk to a teacher or other staff member about academic issues | 71% | 35% | 48% |
| Percentage of students reporting being teased or bothered by other students is a moderate to big hassle | 5% | 17.6% | 11% |
| Percentage of teachers who report that at least weekly teachers examine students' work to guide instruction | 71% | 36.6% | 46% |

*Source:* Rhode Island Department of Education Statistics, 2006–2007 (http://www.ride.ri.gov)

testing system for Grades 2–11 called STAR (Standardized Testing and Reporting), and a high school exit exam called CAHSEE (California High School Exit Exam). It also called for measures of school quality like the ones we just cited from Rhode Island; however, California has never implemented what was called for (Education Data Partnership, 2008). Both the testing systems the state has implemented are based on the California Content Standards, and produce student-level and school-level data disaggregated by student subgroups. The STAR tests are subject specific, for example, Algebra I and U.S. History/Geography, but are low-stakes tests for students in the sense that they do not affect grades or promotion. However, they do constrain the curriculum, as we point out below. CAHSEE is a test of reading, writing, and math and is a high-stakes pass/fail test for students. All California students take it in the 10th grade, and then have three more chances to pass it (retaking only those sections they have not yet passed). The statewide class of 2008 had a cumulative pass rate by their graduation date of 90.2%. This overall pass rate masks significantly lower rates for African Americans (80.1%), English-language learners (72.8%), and students who had received special education services (53.8%).

Both these testing systems feed into the determination of a California school's status under state accountability rules, and then into the determination of school and also district AYP status under NCLB. This all begins with the calculation by the California Department of Education of a statistic derived from a school's spring test results. It is called the Academic Performance Index (API) and is a single number on a scale from 200 to 1000. The State Board of Education set 800 as the API goal for every school and uses a 2-year testing cycle to gauge progress in meeting this goal. Schools receive their base API score in March, before the spring testing cycle. Thus in March 2008, for example, schools received "base scores" calculated on spring 2007 test scores. Then in September 2008, they received "growth scores" calculated on the spring 2008 test scores. Schools are expected to close the gap between their original base score and the 800 target by 5% a year, or a minimum of 5 points. Schools above 800 are expected to stay there. Their progress is publicly reported each year not just in terms of API points risen or fallen, but also in terms of how their API stands in relation to all other high schools in the state (statewide rank), and in relation to a group of 100 schools from around the state with similar student characteristics (similar school rank). These ranks are reported in a number from 1 to 10 (with "1" designating the lowest 10th).

AYP for California high schools is determined by testing participation rate, graduation rate, API, and percentage of students proficient as measured by subgroup performances on CAHSEE. The targets increase each year, headed toward the magical 2014. So, for example, the 2008–9 proficiency target on the ELA portion of CAHSEE is 33.4%. But in 2009–10, it will rise to 44.5%—on its way to 100% by 2013–14. As you will note below in the table of statistics we present, the impact of NCLB on the different kind of high schooling that BP promotes is currently no more severe in California than in Rhode Island. However, because of NCLB particularly, the path ahead for high schools that are different is dangerous in both states.

There are currently seven BP schools in California. Of these, two have just opened (as of fall 2008), of which one is a continuation school that operates on a different accountability system. This leaves five schools (see Table 6.5). We include a column for statewide API rank in the table, though the state warns on its Web site that this statistic is unreliable for small schools (http://ayp.cde.ca.gov/reports). We do not include a column for

**Table 6.5.** NCLB indicators in California: comparing five Big Picture schools with a set of selected comparison schools in the same community

| Schools | Graduation rate in 2008* | API growth rate in 2008 | API statewide rank in 2008 | Met AYP in 2008 | Comparison (based on 2007 data) |
|---|---|---|---|---|---|
| School 1 | 83.3% | 689 (+55) | 2 | Yes | When compared with 13 other high schools in this city, this one is 10th from the top in API, 2nd from the top in ELA, 10th from the top in math. It is one of 9 high schools to make AYP. |
| School 2 | 100% | 661 (–40) | 5 | Yes | When compared with 110 other high schools in this city, this one is 25th from the top in API, 24th in ELA, 12th in math. It is one of 39 high schools in the city to make AYP. |
| School 3 | 100% | 782 (+88) | 5 | Yes | This is classified as an alternative high school. When compared with 40 other high schools in this city (both regular and alternative), this one is 15th from the top in API; 7th from the top in ELA; 8th from the top in math. It is one of 30 high schools in the city to make AYP. |
| School 4 | 93.1% | 719 (–3) | 6 | Yes | This is the only small school among 7 in the county. When compared to the other 7, it is 7th in API, ELA, and math. However, it is above the state average in all these measures. It is one of the 6 high schools in the county to make AYP. |
| School 5 | 87.1% | 571 (–24) | 2 | No | When compared with 31 other high schools in this city, it is 18th from the top in AYP, and 9th in both ELA and math. It is one of only 10 high schools in the city to make AYP. |

* Note that graduation rates in small high schools may fluctuate dramatically from year to year, given the small number of students enrolled. Thus, for example, the graduation rates in 2007 for schools 1 and 4 were each 100%, and that for school 5 was 96%.

*Sources:* California Department of Education (www.cde.ca.gov) and Education Data Partnership (www.ed-data.k12.ca.us).

the similar schools rank, since the state does not calculate this for small schools. Still, as we pointed out above, getting the right comparison group is crucial for evaluating BP school data. We have therefore constructed our own comparisons. In four cases—all city schools—we chose all the other high schools in the city as the comparison group (just as we did above for Rhode Island). In the fifth case, however, we chose (with less validity to the comparison) all the other high schools in this rural county. Note that in making these comparisons, we had to rely on 2007 data since some 2008 data was not yet available as the book went to press.

California sets API growth targets for its schools each year based on their distance from 800, but the tests that underpin API are not growth based. That is, different students take them each year. Nonetheless, when school populations are large, their test scores (and derived API) may be expected to remain relatively stable year to year. Thus changes in teaching can be more validly associated with changes in test scores. However, the total enrollments of the schools whose data are represented in this table range from 131 to 145. This smallness makes their scores highly susceptible to fluctuation—whether upward by 88 points, or downward by 44—and not good indicators of improvement or decline in school quality. Similarly, school number 5 missed AYP in 2008 by failing one criterion (API), but was among the third of all high schools in its city to make AYP the previous year—as the comparison cell above indicates—and was also in the top third that year in terms of ELA and math proficiency. Is the failure to make AYP in 2008 the result of decline or fluctuation? One purpose of this kind of measurement is to invite investigation of such questions, by school and district leaders, faculty, parents, and others. However, "failing to make adequate yearly progress" is a judgmental phrase that tends instead to cut off investigation and to spur what may be unwarranted interventions.

## WHAT WE MEASURE WHEN WE MEASURE "PROFICIENCY"

Let's begin by looking at NECAP, the tristate standards and assessment system in use in Rhode Island. It may seem at first like a tristate NAEP, but it's not. NAEP is the National Assessment of Education Progress, often referred to as the nation's report card. It is a low-stakes assessment that serves participating states as a kind of barometer of the academic rigor of their overall schooling and assessment systems. NAEP uses a sampling strategy that allows it to report national data, as well as state- and district-level data for those states and districts that wish to participate. The data it produces are useful for guiding investments, for example, in the construction of science labs, the education of math teachers, or the teaching of history and writing. Because it does not produce school- or student-level data, however, it steers clear of imposing the kind of curricular conformity that NECAP threatens. And NECAP's power in this regard is much greater inasmuch as it ties into the accelerating pressures of NCLB. If the successor federal law to NCLB continues the march toward presumed "proficiency" in 2014, testing systems like NECAP could wipe out the kind of differences in high school that we think the United States needs.

NECAP tests are curriculum based, tied to a framework of grade-span expectations. To understand the constraints this creates for high school difference, consider two examples of these grade-span expectations, one in math, the other in reading:

> By the end of grade 10, a student "makes and defends conjectures, constructs geometric arguments, uses geometric properties, or uses theorems to solve problems involving angles, lines, polygons, circles, or right angle ratios (sine, cosine, tangent) within mathematics" (NECAP Grade Span Expectations in Mathematics for grades 9–12, 2006 Final Version, http://www.ride.ri.gov).
>
> By the end of grade 10, students "analyze and interpret author's craft, citing evidence where appropriate by demonstrating knowledge of author's style or use of literary elements and devices (i.e. imagery, repetition, flashback, foreshadowing, personification, hyperbole, symbolism, *analogy, allusion, diction, syntax*, or use of punctuation) to analyze literary works" (NECAP Grade Span Expectations in Reading, grades 5–12, 2006 Final Version, http://www.ride.ri.gov).

Note the implicit reliance here on a traditional curriculum sequence, holding, for example, that trigonometric functions are covered in Grade 10, or that what ought to distinguish 11th graders from 9th graders in their literary skills is an understanding of analogy, allusion, diction, and syntax (the reason these words are highlighted in the standard). *By design*, the Met cannot adopt such traditional curricular sequences. The Met especially targets students who have not previously found success in traditional curricular sequences—students much like the 97% of 11th graders attending non-exam-based high schools in Providence who fell below proficiency on the 2007 NECAP math exam. Ultimately, the problem with NECAP exams is that they overdetermine *proficiency*. Who says that being a proficient young adult reader means knowing how to recognize allusion and characterize diction? This is an *academic* distinction, not an *intellectual* one. It is certainly possible to be an intellectually proficient adult reader in the real world and not be able to do these things. Deborah Meier suggests that we often confuse the intellectual with the academic, producing a trap that catches many American youth, particularly in urban areas. We think that this trap accounts substantially for the high dropout rate in these areas.

Does this mean that we should never teach about allusion and diction, and never test for knowledge of them? Of course not. However, when we associate high schooling so closely with teaching and learning such specific concepts and skills, we diminish the prospects for inventing and maintaining high schooling paths that take a broader view.

In a 2005 speech to the National Governors' Association, Bill Gates cited the Met and High Tech High as examples of the different kind of high school needed to address what he described as the obsolescence of the conventional model, and he used the principles of *rigor*, *relevance*, and *relationships* as the standard. But how to judge what meets the standard among all possible alternative designs? The mix of metrics he used in this regard are interesting:

> Two years ago, I visited High Tech High in San Diego. It was conceived in 1998 by a group of San Diego business leaders who became alarmed by the city's shortage of talented high-tech workers. Thirty-five percent of High Tech High students are black or Hispanic. All of them study courses like computer animation and biotechnology in the school's state-of-the-art labs. High Tech High's scores on statewide academic tests are 15 percent higher than the rest of the district; their SAT scores are an average of 139 points higher.
>
> At the Met School in Providence, Rhode Island, 70 percent of the students are black or Hispanic. More than 60 percent live below the poverty line. Nearly 40 percent come from families where English is a second language. As part of its special mission, the Met enrolls only students who have dropped out in the past or were in danger of dropping out. Yet, even with this student body, the Met now has the lowest dropout rate and the highest college placement rate of any high school in the state. (Gates, 2005, online)

We like the pragmatism of this mix of metrics. Figuring out what works well requires multiple measures thoughtfully weighed with some principles in mind about what ought to matter. More about this in the final section of this chapter.

Meanwhile, in California, the same constraint holds. At the heart of the California accountability system are the California Content Standards. These standards, first devised (amid much political turmoil) in the 1990s, are long lists of concepts and skills organized by grade span or subject (for example, English Language Arts Grades 11 and 12, or Algebra 1). They are comparable to the NECAP standards quoted above. Here is a taste—this for ELA Grades 11 and 12:

> 3.6 Analyze the way in which authors through the centuries have used archetypes drawn from myth and tradition in literature, film, political speeches, and religious writings (e.g., how the archetypes of banishment from an ideal

world may be used to interpret Shakespeare's tragedy *Macbeth*) (California State Board of Education, 1997, p. 67)

California supplements its content standards with what are called Curriculum Frameworks. These are massive guides to teaching with the content standards in mind. The Reading/Language Arts Framework is 386 pages long, and the Math Framework is 411 pages. What we find interesting about the frameworks—from the perspective of the Mindset Challenge— is the content continuity they presume from kindergarten through 12th grade. Here, for example, are some excerpts from the Reading/Language Arts Curriculum Framework (California State Board of Education, 2007):

> The standards for the eleventh and twelfth grades are the *pinnacle* [our emphasis] of all the standards for the language arts. Most of the standards at this level are sophisticated extensions of the knowledge and skills previously targeted in the earlier grades. (p. 231)

> In some cases standards address new goals, such as mastering appropriate interviewing techniques. Regardless, emphasis continues to be centered on analyzing literature in greater depth, analyzing career-related and other informational discourse, completing more complex writing assignments, and giving more extensive oral presentations. (p. 212)

> By the twelfth grade students are expected each year to read independently two million words of running text . . . a logical extension of the eighth-grade goal of one million words. (p. 210)

By contrast, BP high schooling presumes *dis*continuity between the lower grades and high school. It deliberately switches the intellectual orientation of high schooling from the disciplines to the occupations. It does so not just to benefit students for whom earlier schooling along disciplinary routes was not smooth travel, but also as a matter of principle. It aims to gain rigor from relevance rather than from disciplinary alignment. This is the BP difference. The fact that the California accountability system, like the Rhode Island one, is built on a different basis is a problem that will grow worse as 2014 approaches and will likely remain a Mindset Challenge even if NCLB goes away. Unless, that is, we also make other kinds of changes.

## HOW TO ESCAPE THE DOUBLE BIND

In this chapter, we have argued that the American high school is in a double bind. It is being asked to prepare all students for higher education and a knowledge-dependent workplace, but also keep some design features it would need to change in order to do this. These features go well beyond large impersonal size. They also include an organizational fixation on classrooms, which, like the fixation of hospitals on beds, induces client passivity. And they include the singleminded focus on discipline-based knowledge that is characteristic of high school curriculum and testing and that causes some substantial fraction of youth to tune out.

Nor will a simpleminded "back to the future" approach to high schooling remove the double bind. Yes, designs for different kinds of high schooling can help, but only if we can figure out how to ensure that the youth they serve are indeed all *high* schooled, and only if the measures we use to ensure this don't punish the schools for being different. Certainly we don't need academies for sewing and gunnery in this century, any more than we need comprehensive high schools that track students by their presumed "abilities." On the other hand, we cannot have—nor should we want to strive for—the kind of high schools that NCLB projects for 2014. It's not that NCLB has the wrong goal, but it surely has the wrong strategy for reaching it.

So what is to be done? One of the best answers we have ever heard to this question came in a speech to a packed ballroom in Chicago during the 2007 American Educational Research Association (AERA) annual meeting. The AERA annual meeting has only one event in its weeklong program each year when no other events are scheduled. This is when the association's president speaks. In 2007, the president was Eva Baker, psychologist and psychometrician, distinguished professor at UCLA, and longtime director of the National Center for Research on Evaluation, Standards, and Student Testing. Baker's speech began auspiciously, we thought (our minds on BP):

> This talk—"The End(s) of Testing"—is about balance in testing. It is about what we have now, ways to move to a new equilibrium, and where we reconnect achievement to learning, equity to more than equal test scores, and students to their own paths. (Baker, 2007, p. 309)

In speaking about "what we have now," Baker quoted Jerome Bruner (1996) on the need to balance the institutional and the personal in education. She argued that "accountability tests have swung education strongly toward institutional goals and away from those of the individual." She was careful to acknowledge the legitimate role that such tests play in "the redress of inadequate or inequitable outcomes," but she added that for secondary schools in the United States especially, they now hold too much sway.

After noting the many efforts to "mitigate" the bad side effects of standardized testing—to make it performance-based or technology-based, to use multiple measures, to add formative dimensions, to create tests worth teaching to, and so on—she called in the end for just leaving the tests alone. "They are resilient and embedded in our traditions," she said, "and changes to them are always temporary (they snap back like rubber bands), with trivial residues at best." But have fewer of them, she added, make sure the ones we have are actually valid, and fix No Child Left Behind. Then she argued for going beyond standardized testing in thinking about accountability at the high school level and to make room for the personal as well as the institutional in designing for accountability (p. 309). "Can we have balance and deal with the students we have now without wishing they were different?" she asked. "Can we offer students options better suited to a new and changing work environment, to a life in real-time society with amped-up connectivity? And can we teach them in a way that models flexibility and problem solving?" (p. 313).

Answering these rhetorical questions, she proposed a system of Qualifications, modeled on those already in place in other nations. She described a Qualification as "a validated accomplishment, obtained inside or *outside* school." The italics are our emphasis, meant to signify that the system Baker advocates follows Ted Sizer's (2004) advice cited above to unlearn our habit of thinking of education only in terms of schools. Baker's proposed system also follows Nel Noddings's (1992) advice, again cited above, to replace a single ideal of the educated person with multiple ideals tuned to the multiplicity of human capacities and interests. Students choose the Qualifications they go after. The way a student obtains a Qualification may resemble taking a course (for example, an International Baccalaureate course in school or a calculus course at a nearby college, or an art history course at a museum); but it may also involve engaging in a musical or sports performance in or outside school, community service, a science competition, or an arts or business internship; or it may involve the pursuit of a certification (for example, in cardiopulmonary resuscitation, restaurant cooking, or network management). Qualifications, she noted, "should span a range of personal goals and, with any luck, help [students] to develop a passion in at least one area" (p. 313). But they should also be undergirded by what she called an "ontology." For example, each Qualification might require complex and adaptive problem solving and thinking, the building and tending of a rich knowledge base, metacognition, communicative performance, and so on. There are excellent guides available on the different types of thinking about standards that Baker's call for an "ontology" suggests. One is a 1991 report from the United States Department of Labor, known as the SCANS Report (for the commission that produced it, the Secretary's Commission on Achieving Necessary Skills). And we'd recommend three other very useful books: Richard Murnane's and Frank Levy's (1996) *Teaching the New Basic Skills*; William Sedlacek's (2004) *Beyond the Big Test*;

and Tony Wagner's (2008) *The Global Achievement Gap*. All four of these resources urge us to rethink what we called above (after Deborah Meier) the tendency of education to substitute the merely academic for the intellectual. Without denying the important role in education of the disciplines, they suggest that high schooling in particular has to pay at least equal attention to life—particularly life in the 21st-century economy.

# 7

# The Road Map

This chapter is the road map (that doesn't fold out). Here we recapitulate the challenges we explored in the first six chapters, and say in a nutshell what we think you ought to do to manage them. Of course, the challenges are especially relevant to the task of going to scale with new school designs. But we think most apply also (by means of analogy and reflection) to many other kinds of school change.

In the book, we explored eight challenges. We called five of them the *first* challenges. They deal with the fundamental question of what the design is. We explored these in Chapters 2 and 3. Then we explored, in Chapters 4, 5, and 6 respectively, three other complicated challenges. Our road map below follows the same plan.

## HITTING THE ROAD: THE FIRST CHALLENGES

### THE FIDELITY CHALLENGE: BALANCING FIDELITY AND ADAPTATION

- Remember that the Fidelity Challenge is a dilemma and that you have to give due deference to both of its poles. Absolute fidelity will crack under contextual pressures. On the other hand, too much adaptation can easily erase the design.
- Figure out how to maximize both fidelity and adaptation—the "both/and" approach. Do this by subordinating both to the core vision.
- Articulate the design's core elements. Without this articulation, you will not know what to be faithful to, or what to adapt.
- Force yourself to say what practices would "step over the line," or be antithetical to the design and its core vision.

### THE TEACHING CHALLENGE: TEACHING AND LEARNING THE DESIGN

- Cultivate design experts and help them become teachers of the design. Remember that expertise is necessary but not sufficient to good teaching.

- Understand that learning the design means unlearning some other design.
- Create images of the design in action—visual, verbal, interactive, live, and virtual.
- Make the design transparent, so that people who want to learn it can figure it out on contact.

### THE OWNERSHIP CHALLENGE:
### INSTILLING SHARED OWNERSHIP OF THE DESIGN

- Remember that ownership comes from taking risks.
- Design experiences that immerse newcomers in the culture of the design but leave them space to act "as if."
- Train newcomers to become experts in the design.
- Be willing in the end to "hand over the keys" to the people you've trained.

### THE COMMUNICATION CHALLENGE:
### COMMUNICATING EFFECTIVELY ACROSS CONTEXTS

- Expect communication strain going to scale. One of the first manifestations will be strain on the intimacy of knowledge exchange between new adopters and the home office.
- Use all the tools you can afford to ease the strain: Internet, intranet, video-conferencing, podcasting, and so on. Better to be redundant than skimp. However, be wary of "overcommunication" (using "telling" to control).
- Think about coaching as a communication tool. Coaches are the jump drives of the design. They take it *out there* and watch and listen as *it* and *there* intersect. Then they bring it home to upload changes.

### THE FEEDBACK CHALLENGE:
### USING EXPERIENCE IN NEW SETTINGS TO IMPROVE THE DESIGN

- Nurture communities of practice, the groups that work together to make the design work well locally. Think of them as the brains of the design.
- Connect them to each other to spread learning and innovation.
- Train leaders to facilitate communities of practice and also networks of practice.

## WATCH OUT FOR RESOURCE COMPLICATIONS

### THE RESOURCE CHALLENGE: GETTING THEM

- You need three resources: money, smart people, and cutting-edge ideas.

- Act "rashly" to build resources, and use slack to cover inevitable pockets of deficit.
- Consider even the smallest resource gain an investment in future gains.
- Connect, connect. Every connection is a potential resource gain.

### The Resource Challenge: Managing Them

- Make plans early to consult with experts in the design of financial systems, human resource management systems, and information and communication systems.
- Think of strategic planning as ongoing, inevitably provisional, and crucial.
- Expect local resource emergencies, and plan to deploy central resources to fill the gaps.
- Build action research capacity into the school design itself and into coaching for implementation.
- Imagine and use rich indicator systems—even if it takes years to get them right.
- Network for accountability as well as communication.

### The Resource Challenge: Going to Scale

- Keep all systems nimble, and expect to change them frequently as you grow—particularly communication systems and management systems.
- Expect organizational turbulence as a result, and figure out how to talk openly about its sources.
- Do not assume that growth is a steadily upward curve. Look for the right curve.
- Be bold in taking the steps you need to keep the vision intact.
- Be realistic about the job demands of site-level leadership, and tailor training and support mechanisms accordingly.
- Design for cost sharing, and help schools budget for it.

## POLITICAL ADVENTURES JUST AHEAD

### The Political Challenge: Starting Up

- Get clear about what you espouse and why.
- Expect that local politics will work to distort your intentions and designs.

- Find out about this kind of distortion in other situations, and learn how people in your position managed to counteract it.
- Take advantage of your initial status as an outsider on the inside to learn the local politics from people who know it.
- Map out the groups who have the power to help you or hurt you, and determine what power resources you can marshal and connect with.
- Reach a political understanding—as *understanding* is defined in the local culture. Make this the basis of contractual negotiation.
- In negotiations, pin down as many details as possible, leaving maximal room for design changes and for start-up and growing pains.

### THE POLITICAL CHALLENGE: LATER ON

- Expect incoherence in the policies that bear on your work. Act wherever possible to reduce the incoherence.
- Look continually for opportunities to do whatever you can to make a place for your school and its different design in the political context.
- Know how to resolve conflicts by assessing and addressing parties' basic interests. Practice the skill whenever and wherever you can.
- Keep explaining your school again and again: how it works, and what it values. Learn to do this in 30 seconds or less. Say why it matters to the nation as well as the community.
- Affiliate, affiliate—but know that you must work hard to make each affiliation a source of strength and advantage.
- Remember that politics is all about who has leverage and is willing to use it. Get some, and use it.
- Understand that no design is adopted without adaptation. Go for optimal adaptation—one that protects the school and enables it to gain influence, but also maintains the design's integrity.
- Above all, stay engaged politically.

## DANGER: THE DIFFERENCE THAT DIFFERENCE MAKES

### THE MINDSET CHALLENGE: ESCAPING THE DOUBLE BIND

- Expand your idea of who the kids are, and get a "bigger picture" of high school life.
- Unlearn the tendency to have one model of the ideal education. We need multiple models.
- Unlearn schoolcentric accountability. It takes a village to be accountable.

- When you think about high school, think about high schooling—still *high*, but as varied in goals and design as real-world intellectual adventures are.
- Do whatever you can, whatever your role, to change the accountability systems in American schooling to make room for the personal as well as the institutional.

# References

Alternative High School Initiative. (n.d.). Retrieved August 27, 2007, from http://www.ahsi.info/mission.htm.

Angus, D., & Mirel, J. (1999). *The failed promise of the American high school, 1890–1995.* New York: Teachers College Press.

Argyris, C., & Schön, D. (1978), *Organizational learning: A theory of action.* Reading, MA: Addison-Wesley.

Argyris, C., & Schön, D. A. (1996). *Organizational learning II: Theory, method, and practice.* Reading, MA: Addison-Wesley.

Baker, E. L. (2007). The end(s) of testing: Presidential address to the American Educational Research Association Annual Meeting. *Educational Researcher, 36*(6), 309–317.

Berends, M., Bodilly, S. J., & Kirby, S. N. (2002*). Facing the challenges of whole-school reform: New American schools after a decade.* Washington, DC: Rand.

Bolman, L. G., & Deal, T. E. (1997). *Reframing organizations: Artistry, choice, and leadership* (2nd ed.). San Francisco: Jossey-Bass.

Boyer, E. L. (1985). *High school: A report on secondary education in America.* New York: HarperCollins.

Bransford, J., Brown, A., & Cocking, R. (2000). *How people learn: Brain, mind, and experience and school.* Washington, DC: National Academy Press.

Bremer, J., & von Moschzisker, M. (1971). *The school without walls: Philadelphia's Parkway Program.* New York: Holt, Rinehart, & Winston.

Brokaw, L. (2003, January). Case study: Local heroes. *Hemispheres,* 34–36, 59.

Brown, J. S., & Gray, E. S. (1995, November). The people are the company: How to build your company around your people. *Fast Company.* Retrieved January 11, 2009, from http://www.fastcompany.com/magazine/01/people.html

Bruner, J. (1996). *The culture of education.* Cambridge, MA: Harvard University Press.

Burlingham, B. (2003, January). The coolest small company in America. *Inc Magazine,* retrieved January 12, 2009, from http://www.inc.com/magazine/20030101/25036.html.

Burlingham, B. (2005). *Small giants: Companies that choose to be great instead of big.* New York: Penguin.

California State Board of Education. (1997, December). *English-language arts content standards for California public schools, kindergarten through grade twelve.* Sacramento, CA: Author.

California State Board of Education. (2007). *Reading/language arts framework for California public schools, kindergarten through grade twelve.* Sacramento, CA: Author.

Carnoy, M., Elmore, R., & Siskin, L. S. (2003). *The new accountability: High schools and high-stakes testing.* New York: Routledge Falmer.

Chubb, J. E. (2004). The first few years of Edison Schools: Ten lessons in getting to scale. In Glennan, T. K., Bodilly, S. W., Galegher, J. R., & Kerr, K. (Eds.), *Expanding the reach of education reforms* (pp. 487–516). Santa Monica: Rand.

Clark, R. W., Foster, A. M., & Mantle-Bromley, C. (2006). In K. R. Howey & N. Zimpher (Eds.), *Boundary spanners* (pp. 27–46). Washington, DC: American Association of State Colleges and Universities, and the National Association of State Universities and Land-Grant Colleges.

Cohen, B., & Greenfield, J. (1997). *Ben & Jerry's double-dip.* New York: Simon & Schuster.

Cohen, D. K., & Neufeld, B. (1981). The failure of high schools and the progress of education. *Daedulus, 110,* 69–89.

Collins, J., & Porras, J. (1994). *Built to last: Successful habits of visionary companies.* New York: Harper Business.

Collins, J., & Porras, J. (2001). *Good to great: Why some companies make the leap—and others don't.* New York: Harper Business.

Conant, J. B. (1959). *The American high school today: A first report to interested citizens.* New York: McGraw-Hill.

Conant, J. B. (1960). *The child, the parent, and the state.* Cambridge, MA: Harvard University Press.

Csikszentmihalyi, M., & Schneider, B. (2000). *Becoming adult: How teenagers prepare for the world of work.* New York: Basic Books.

Daggett, W. R. (2005). *Rigor and relevance from concept to reality.* Rexford, NY: International Center for Leadership in Education.

Darling-Hammond, L. (2007, May 2). Evaluating "No Child Left Behind." *The Nation.* Retrieved January 11, 2009, from http://www.thenation.com/doc/20070521/darling-hammond/single

Datnow, A., Hubbard, L., & Mehan, H. (2001). *Extending educational reform from one school to many.* New York: Routledge.

Davenport, T. H., & Prusak, L. (1998). *Working knowledge.* Boston: Harvard Business School Press.

Dees, G. (2001). Mobilizing resources. In J. G. Dees, J. Emerson, & P. Economy (Eds.), *Enterprising nonprofits: A toolkit for social entrepreneurs* (pp. 63–102). New York: John Wiley & Sons.

Dees, J. G., Emerson, J., & Economy, P. (2001). *Enterprising nonprofits: A toolkit for social entrepreneurs.* New York: John Wiley & Sons.

Dewey, J. (1938/1997). *Experience and education.* New York: Touchstone.

*Digest of Educational Statistics.* (2000). Chapter 2, elementary and secondary education, Table 99. Washington, DC: National Center for Educational Statistics.

Dillon, S. (2007, December 23). Democrats make Bush school act an election issue. *New York Times,* retrieved January 11, 2009, from http://www.nytimes.com/

2007/12/23/us/politics/23child.html?_r=1&scp=1&sq=Democrats%20make%20Bush%20school%20act%20an%20election%20issue%20&st=cse

Education Data Partnership. (2008, May). *Understanding the Academic Performance Index*. Retrieved July 19, 2008, from www.ed-data.k12.ca.us

*Education Week.* (2008). *EPE Research Center.* Retrieved September 26, 2008, from http://www.edweek.org/rc

Expeditionary Learning Schools. (2007). *Evidence of success summary: 2007.* New York: Author.

Featherstone, J. (1971). *Schools where children learn*. New York: Liveright.

Fishman, C. (1996, April). Whole Foods is all team. *Fast Company 2*, p. 103.

Flanigan, J. (2006, February 16). Venture capitalists are investing in educational reform. *New York Times*, retrieved January 11, 2009, from http://www.nytimes.com/2006/02/16/business/16sbiz.html?scp=1&sq=%22Venture%20capitalists%20are%20investing%20in%20educational%20reform&st=cse

Flavin, M. (1996). *Kurt Hahn's school and legacy: To discover you can be more and do more than you believed*. Wilmington, DE: Middle Atlantic Press.

Florida, R. (2002). Bohemia and economic geography. *Journal of Economic Geography*, 2(1), (2), 55–71.

Friedenberg, E. Z. (1964). *Coming of age in America*. New York: Random House.

Friedenberg, E. Z. (1965). *The dignity of youth and other atavisms*. Boston: Beacon Press.

Friedman, M. (1955). The role of government in education. In R. A. Solo (Ed.), *Economics and the public interest* (pp. 123–144). Piscataway, NJ: Rutgers University Press.

Gates, B. (2005, February 26). Prepared remarks to the National Governors Association/Achieve Summit. Retrieved August 16, 2008, from http://www.nga.org/cda/files/es05gates.pdf

Gladwell, M. (2000). *The tipping point*. New York: Little, Brown.

Gleason, P. (1995). *Contending with modernity: Catholic higher education in twentieth-century America*. New York: Oxford University Press.

Glennan, T. K. (1998). *New American schools after six years*. Washington, DC: Rand.

Glennan, T. K., Bodilly, S. J., Galegher, J. R., & Kerr, K. A. (2004). *Expanding the reach of education reforms: Perspectives from leaders in the scale-up of educational interventions*. Santa Monica, CA: Rand.

Goldberg, C. (1999, December 22). Vermonters would keep lid on Ben & Jerry's pint. *New York Times*, retrieved January 12, 2009, from http://query.nytimes.com/gst/fullpage.html?res=940CE2D61639F931A15751C1A96F958260

Goodlad, J. I. (1984). *A place called school*. New York: McGraw-Hill.

Goodman, P. (1964). *Compulsory mis-education*. New York: Horizon Press.

Gootman, E. (2004, March 3). Many at successful middle school oppose its expansion. *The New York Times*, retrieved January 11, 2009, from http://query.nytimes.com/gst/fullpage.html?res=9E0CE2D9153FF930A35750C0A9629C8B63&scp=1&sq=%22Many+at+successful+middle+school+oppose+its+expansion%22&st=nyt

Grossman, P. L., Wineburg, S., & Woolworth, S. (2001, December). Toward a theory of teacher community. *Teachers College Record*, *103*(6), 942–1012.

Hammack, F. M. (Ed.). (2004). *The comprehensive high school today*. New York: Teachers College Press.

Hampel, R. (1986). *The last little citadel: American high schools since 1940*. Boston: Houghton Mifflin.

Hays, C. L. (2000, April 13). Ben & Jerry's to Unilever with attitude. *New York Times*, retrieved January 11, 2009, from http://query.nytimes.com/gst/fullpage.html?res=9404E3D7133EF930A25757C0A9669C8B63

Hildreth, P., & Kimble, C. (Eds.). (2004). *Knowledge networks: Innovation through communities of practice*. York, UK: IGI.

Hoff, D. J. (2007, December 19). Amid pessimism on NCLB, talks continue. *Education Week*, retrieved January 12, 2009, from http://www.edweek.org/ew/articles/2007/12/19/16nclb.h27.html?qs=Amid%20Pessimism%20on%20NCLB,%20Talks%20Continue

Holt, J. (1964). *How children fail*. New York: Pittman.

Holt, J. (1967). *How children learn*. New York: Pittman.

Howey, K. R., & Zimpher, N. L. (Eds.). (2006). *Boundary spanners*. Washington, DC: American Association of State Colleges and Universities, and National Association of State Universities and Land-Grant Colleges.

Illich, I. (1971). *Deschooling society*. New York: Harper & Row.

Kammeraad-Campbell, S. (1989). *Doc: The story of Dennis Littky and his fight for a better school*. New York: NTC/Contemporary.

Keltner, B. R. (1998). Funding comprehensive school reform [Rand Issue Paper]. Retrieved January 11, 2009, from http://wwwcgi.rand.org/pubs/issue_papers/IP175/index2.html

Kitzi, J. (2001). Recognizing and assessing new opportunities. In J. G. Dees, J. Emerson, & P. Economy, (Eds.), *Enterprising nonprofits: A toolkit for social entrepreneurs* (pp. 43–62). New York: John Wiley & Sons.

Klein, E. J. (2005). Theory into practice: Professional development design and implementation in a small high school development project. *Dissertation Abstracts International, 66*(02), 475A. (UMI No. 3166531).

Krug, E. A. (1964). *The shaping of the American high school*. New York: Harper & Row.

Krug, E. A. (1972). *The shaping of the American high school, volume 2, 1920–1941*. Madison: University of Wisconsin Press.

Labaree, D. F. (1988). *The making of an American high school: The credentials market and the Central High School of Philadelphia, 1838–1939*. New Haven: Yale University Press.

Lager, F. (1994). *Ben & Jerry's: The inside scoop—How two real guys built a business with a social conscience and a sense of humor*. New York: Crown.

Lave, J., & Wenger, E. (1991). *Situated learning: Legitimate peripheral participation*. New York: Cambridge University Press.

Lee, V. E., & Ready, D. D. (2006). *Schools within schools: Possibilities and pitfalls of high school reform*. New York: Teachers College Press.

Levine, E. (2002). *One kid at a time: Big lessons from a small school*. New York: Teachers College Press.

Lipsitz, J. (1984). *Successful schools for young adolescents*. New Brunswick, NJ: Transaction Books.

Littky, D. (with S. Grabelle). (2004). *The big picture: Education is everyone's business*. Alexandria, VA: Association for Supervision and Curriculum Development.

Magliozzi, T., & Magliozzi, R. (2000). *In our humble opinion: Car Talk's Click and Clack rant and rave*. New York: Berkeley.

Margolick, D. (2008, July). Tall order. *Conde Nast Portfolio*, pp. 68–77, 120–123.

McDonald, J. P. (2004). High school in the 21st century: Managing the core dilemma. In F. M. Hammack (Ed.), *The comprehensive high school today* (pp. 26–44). New York: Teachers College Press.

McDonald, J. P., Buchanan, J., & Sterling, R. (2004). The National Writing Project: Scaling up and scaling down. In T. K. Glennan, S. J. Bodilly, J. R. Galegher, & K. A. Kerr (Eds.), *Expanding the reach of education reforms* (pp. 81–105). Washington, DC: Rand.

McDonald, J. P., Klein, E. J., & Riordan, M. (in collaboration with S. Broun). (2003a, February). *Scaling up the Big Picture* (*essay 1*). Unpublished manuscript, New York University.

McDonald, J. P., Klein, E. J., & Riordan, M. (in collaboration with S. Broun). (2003b, June). *Scaling up the Big Picture* (*essay 2*). Unpublished manuscript, New York University.

McDonald, J. P., Klein, E. J., & Riordan, M. (2004a, February). *Scaling up the Big Picture* (*essay 3*). Unpublished manuscript, New York University.

McDonald, J. P., Klein, E. J., & Riordan, M. (2004b, August). *Scaling up the Big Picture* (*essay 4*). Unpublished manuscript, New York University.

McDonald, J. P., Mohr, N., Dichter, A., & McDonald, E. (2007). *The power of protocols: An educator's guide to better practice* (rev. ed.). New York: Teachers College Press.

McGregor, J. (2005, February). Gospels of failure: The reports on three high-profile disasters offer rich lessons in why organizations fail—and how not to. *Fast Company Magazine, 91*(62). Retrieved January 12, 2009, from http://www.fastcompany.com/magazine/91/gospels.html

McLaughlin, M. W., & Talbert, J. E. (2001). *Professional communities and the work of high school teaching*. Chicago: University of Chicago Press.

McLaughlin, M. W., & Talbert, J. E. (2006). *Building school-based teacher learning communities*. New York: Teachers College Press.

McMakin, T. (2001). *Bread and butter: What a bunch of bakers taught me about business and happiness*. New York: St. Martin's Press.

McNulty, R. J., & Quaglia, R. J. (2007). Rigor, relevance and relationships. *The School Administrator*, retrieved January 9, 2009, from http://www.aasa.org/publications/saarticledetail.cfm?ItemNumber=9330

Meier, D. (2002). *The power of their ideas: Lessons from America from a small school in Harlem*. Boston: Beacon Press.

Meier, D. (2004, November). Introduction to D. Littky, *The big picture: Education is everyone's business* (pp. vii–xi). Alexandria, VA: Association for Supervision and Curriculum Development.

Meyer, D. (2006). *Setting the table: The transforming power of hospitality in business.* New York: HarperCollins.

Millot, M. D. (2004). Leveraging the market to scale up improvement programs: A fee-for-service primer for foundations and nonprofits. In T. K. Glennan, S. J. Bodilly, J. R. Galegher, & K. A. Kerr (Eds.), *Expanding the reach of education reforms* (pp. 603–646). Washington, DC: Rand.

Moe, T. M. (2001). *Schools, vouchers, and the American public.* Washington, DC: Brookings Institution Press.

Montessori, M. (1966). *The secret of childhood.* New York: Ballantine Books.

Murnane, R. J., & Levy, F. (1996). *Teaching the new basic skills.* New York: The Free Press.

Nathan, J. (1999). *Charter schools: Creating hope and opportunity for American education.* San Francisco: Jossey-Bass.

National Commission on Excellence in Education. (1983). *A nation at risk: The imperative for educational reform.* Washington, DC: Government Printing Office.

Neill, A. S. (1960). *Summerhill.* New York: Hart.

Newmann, F. M., & Wehlage, G. G. (1995). *Successful school restructuring: A report to the public and educators.* Madison: University of Wisconsin, Education Center.

Noddings, N. (1992). *The challenge to care in the schools.* New York: Teachers College Press.

O'Dell, C., & Grayson, C. J., Jr. (with N. Essaides). (1998). *If only we knew what we know.* New York: Simon & Schuster.

Oldenburg, R. (1989). *The great good place: Cafes, coffee shops, community centers, beauty parlors, general stores, bars, hangouts, and how they get you through the day.* New York: Paragon House.

Oldenburg, R. (1991). *The great good place.* New York: Marlowe.

Peterman, F. (2006). Boundary spanning and the creation of future settings. In K. R. Howey & N. Zimpher (Eds.), *Boundary spanners* (pp. 127–142). Washington, DC: American Association of State Colleges and Universities, and the National Association of State Universities and Land-Grant Colleges.

Peters, T J. (1987). *Thriving on chaos.* Knopf: New York.

Phillips, S. (2000). *Alternative schools in New York City.* Presentation to the Seminar on the Future of the Comprehensive High School. New York: New York University.

Powell, A., Farrar, E., & Cohen, D. K. (1985*). The shopping mall high school: Winners and losers in the educational marketplace.* Boston: Houghton Mifflin.

Reese, W. J. (1995). *The origins of the American high school.* New Haven: Yale University Press.

Rhode Island Department of Education (2007, December). *Rhode Island school performance and accountability system, schools, and districts.* Providence, RI: Author.

Riordan, M. (2006). Discovering the core of experiential education: How Big Picture school students learn through internships. *Dissertation Abstracts International,* A66 (12). (UMI No. 3199985).

Roddick, A. (1991). *Body and soul: Profits with principles.* New York: Crown.

Rumizen, M. C. (2002). *The complete idiot's guide to knowledge management.* Madison, WI: CWL.

Rury, J. L. (2004). The problems of educating urban youth: James B. Conant and the changing context of metropolitan America, 1945–1995. In F. M. Hammack (Ed.), *The comprehensive high school today* (pp. 45–68). New York: Teachers College Press.

Sarason, S. (1972). *The creation of settings and the future societies.* San Francisco: Jossey-Bass.

Sarason, S. (1982). *The culture of the school and the problem of change* (2nd ed.). Boston: Allyn & Bacon.

Sarason, S. (1995). *Charter schools: Another flawed reform?* San Francisco: Jossey-Bass.

Schank, R. (2000). *Coloring outside the lines: Raising a smarter kid by breaking all the rules.* New York: HarperCollins.

Schön, D. A., & McDonald, J. P. (1998). *Doing what you mean to do in school reform.* Providence, RI: Annenberg Institute for School Reform, Brown University.

The Secretary's Commission on Achieving Necessary Skills. (1991). *What work requires of schools: A SCANS report for America 2000.* Washington, DC: U.S. Department of Labor.

Sedlacek, W. E. (2004). *Beyond the big test: Noncognitive assessment in higher education.* San Francisco: Jossey Bass.

Schultz, H. (with D. J. Yang). (1997). *Pour your heart into it: How Starbucks built a company one cup at a time.* New York: Hyperion.

Senge, P. (1990). *The fifth discipline: The art and practice of the learning organization.* New York: Doubleday.

Silberman, C. E. (1970). *Crisis in the classroom: The remaking of American education.* New York: Random House.

Sizer, T. R. (1964a). *The age of the academies.* New York: Bureau of Publications, Teachers College, Columbia University.

Sizer, T. R. (1964b). *Secondary schools at the turn of the century.* New Haven: Yale University Press.

Sizer, T. R. (1984). *Horace's compromise: The dilemma of the American high school.* Boston: Houghton Mifflin.

Sizer, T. R. (1986). Foreword to R. L. Hampel, *The last little citadel* (pp. ix–xii). Boston: Houghton Mifflin.

Sizer, T. (2004). *The red pencil.* New Haven: Yale University Press.

Spolsky, J. (2000). Strategy letter I: Ben and Jerry's vs. Amazon, *Joel on Software,* www.joelonsoftware.com.

Stigler, J. W., & Hiebert, J. (1999). *The teaching gap: Best ideas from the world's teachers for improving education in the classroom.* New York: The Free Press.

Tucker, M. (2004). Reaching for coherence in school reform: The case of America's Choice. In T. K. Glennan, S. J. Bodilly, J. R. Galegher, & K. A. Kerr, *Expanding the reach of educational reforms* (pp. 197–258). Santa Monica, CA: Rand.

Tyack, D., & Cuban, L. (1983). *Tinkering toward utopia: A century of public school reform.* Cambridge: Harvard University Press.

Tyack, D., Lowe, R., & Hansot, E. (1984*). Public schools in hard times: The Great Depression and recent years.* Cambridge, MA: Harvard University Press.

U.S. Bureau of Education. (1918). *Cardinal principles of secondary education*. Bulletin 1918, number 35, Department of the Interior. Washington, DC: Government Printing Office.

U.S. Census Bureau. (1960). *School enrollment and educational attainment for the United States: 1960*. PC(S1)-20. Washington, DC: U. S. Department of Commerce.

Viteritti, J. P. (1999). *Choosing equality: School choice, the Constitution, and civil society*. Washington, DC: Brookings Institution Press.

Wagner, T. (2008). *The global achievement gap*. New York: Basic.

Walker, E., & McDonald, J. P. (1996). *Documentation/evaluation of the Rhode Island Project: Interim report to the Big Picture Company*. Unpublished paper. Providence, RI: Annenberg Institute for School Reform, Brown University.

Walker, R. (Undated). The business of Blue Man. Retrieved January 11, 2009, from http://www.robwalker.net/contents/as_blueman.html

Washor, E. (2003). Innovative pedagogy and school facilities. DesignShare.com. Retrieved July 18, 2008, from http://www.designshare.com/Researcher/Washor/Pedagogy%20and%20Facilities.pdf

Washor, E., & Mojkowski, C. (2006/2007, December/January). Special topic/What do you mean by rigor? *Educational Leadership, 64*(4), 84–87.

Weeks, D. J. (2003). Rigor, relevance, and relationship: The three R's of the Bill and Melinda Gates Foundation. *Northwest Education Magazine, 9*(2), retrieved January 9, 2009, from http://www.nwrel.org/nwedu/09–02/rigor.asp

Weiss, C. H. (1972). *Evaluation research: Methods for evaluating program effectiveness*. Englewood Cliffs, NJ: Prentice-Hall.

Weiss, C. H. (1995). Nothing as good as good theory: Exploring theory-based evaluation for comprehensive community initiatives for children and families. In J. P. Connell, A. C. Kubisch, L. B. Schorr, & C. H. Weiss (Eds.), *New approaches to evaluating community initiatives: Concepts, methods, and contexts* (pp. 65–92). Washington, DC: Aspen Institute.

Wenger, E. (1998). *Communities of practice: Learning, meaning, and identity*. Cambridge, MA: Cambridge University Press.

Wenger, E., McDermott, R., & Snyder, W. M. (2002). *Cultivating communities of practice: A guide to managing knowledge*. Boston: Harvard Business School Press.

Wheatley, M. J. (1992). *Leadership and the new science*. San Francisco: Berrett-Koehler.

Wilson, F. (1998). *The hand*. New York: Vintage Books.

Zak, D. (2008, July 27). Suspended in time: Why can't Hollywood graduate to a bigger picture of high school life? *Washington Post*, p. M1–M10.

# Index

# About the Authors

**Joseph P. McDonald** is professor of teaching and learning at New York University's Steinhardt School of Culture, Education, and Human Development. His research interests include school reform, school design, and the deep study of teaching, and his practical pursuits include the creation of new settings for teacher education. He is the author or co-author of seven books, including *The Power of Protocols*, *School Reform Behind the Scenes*, *Redesigning School*, and *Teaching: Making Sense of an Uncertain Craft*. Joe lives in New York City and Wareham, Massachusetts, with his wife and colleague Beth and their spunky West Highland terrier.

**Emily J. Klein** is assistant professor at Montclair State University of New Jersey in the Department of Curriculum and Teaching, School of Education and Human Services. She previously taught high school English in New York City, where she developed and implemented interdisciplinary curriculum with the American Social History Project and the New York City Opera Project. She is the author of several articles on high school professional development, building communities of practice, and teacher networks. Emily lives in Nyack, New York, with her husband and son.

**Meg Riordan** is a school designer in New York City for Expeditionary Learning Schools Outward Bound (ELS). She supports four ELS in New York City, working with leadership teams on strategic planning, and with teachers on implementing the ELS design for teaching and learning. She also designs and facilitates regional and national teacher professional development for the ELS network. Her research interests and writing focus on experiential education, internship-based learning, communities of practice, school reform, and teacher professional development. Meg lives in the Woodlawn section of the Bronx with her supportive husband and two energetic vizslas.